Mollie
MAKES

CHRISTMAS

Living and loving a handmade holiday

CONTENTS

PUT YOUR OWN STAMP ON IT!

CUTE CHRISTMAS CHARACTERS

EMBROIDERED EMBELLISHMENTS

HOMEMADE DECORATIONS

DECK THE HALLS!

If you're hooked on crochet, hanker for handmade and would rather create your own unique Christmas than buy from a chain store, then this little book is for you. It perfectly captures the "living and loving handmade" spirit of *Mollie Makes* magazine, celebrating the world of "granny chic".

Featuring over 20 new projects from *Mollie Makes* magazine's favorite designers, *Christmas* showcases a passion for handmade. Inspired in part by the huge online community of creative bloggers, the book reflects the cultural shift taking place toward rediscovering the crafting skills of previous generations. Now we too are recognizing how satisfying for the soul it is to knit, crochet, fold, stitch, and sew. From hand-crafted decorations for the home and Christmas table, to things to make and give as gifts, the book satisfies the growing desire to create something special.

Gretel Parker shares her needle felting skills and creates Christmas cottage tree trinkets – sure to become a treasured family heirloom to be packed away in tissue paper year after year. Another favorite is Cara Medus' fun Santa Kit – crocheted carrots, a mince pie and even a bottle of sherry!

Be thrifty and upcycle unloved books into a star garland, or use pretty Japanese papers to make a miniature Christmas tree – perfect for small space living.

Did I mention Kirsty Neale's adorable felt finger puppets, or Carol Meldrum's knitted beaded baby booties? Finally, if Santa has been very generous this year there's Charlie Moorby's chamois fawn felt appliqué iPad case. Way. Too. Cute.

All the projects are easy to follow with clear step-by-step photographs and instructions, plus handy tips along the way. Many are suitable for beginners, but the *Mollie Makes* ethos is to give it a try and be proud of the end result. We positively embrace imperfection.

Here's to Living and Loving a Handmade Christmas,

Jane

NEEDLE FELT
CHRISTMAS COTTAGES

SIMPLE NEEDLE FELTING IS THE PERFECT WAY TO CREATE A COZY COLLECTION
OF DECORATIONS FOR YOUR TREE. YOU CAN MAKE YOUR LITTLE HOUSES ANY SHAPE
YOU CHOOSE BY SCULPTING LOOSE FIBER ROVING WITH ONE OR TWO NEEDLES,
BUT LIMIT YOUR COLORS FOR A STYLISH CO-ORDINATED LOOK.

HOW TO MAKE ... CHRISTMAS COTTAGES

MATERIALS

MERINO ROVING, SMALL AMOUNTS IN SHADES OF RED, GREEN, AND WHITE

ASSORTMENT OF HEART-SHAPED BUTTONS

SEED BEADS

SMALL JUMP RINGS AND SLIGHTLY LARGER BINDER RINGS

EMBROIDERY FLOSS TO MATCH FIBER COLORS

TRIANGULAR FELTING NEEDLES AND HOLDER, AT LEAST TWO SIZE 40

A FELTING MAT (SPONGE OR BRUSH)

SEWING NEEDLE

TIP
To make variations on the basic cottage, simply roll or fold the fiber into roughly the shape you want before modeling it with your needle. A small house like this should take 3–4 hours to make.

01 Take a length of 18" (46 cm) roving teased out to a strip about 2" (5 cm) wide. Fold the roving strip over and over to make a small oblong roll. This will form the base of the cottage.

02 With two needles in your holder, begin jabbing the fiber using your non-needling hand to hold it in place. Needle felting is simply a form of modeling, so use your fingers and thumb as a guide to make the straight lines of the walls and corner angles. Work all sides equally to get a nice 3D shape.

03 After a while, you will feel the fiber firming up and responding to the needle. Carry on working until you have a small, firm block measuring about 1½ x 1" (4 x 2.5 cm).

04 Now to make the roof. Take about 8" (20cm) of teased out red roving (see step 1) and place it centrally on top of the cottage base. Bunch up a plug of fiber for a bit of extra filling inside and anchor it in with your needles.

05 Fold the edges over and towards the middle in a loose pyramid shape, and begin to shape a little roof, using your fingers and thumb to hold

the fiber in place. Don't forget to keep turning as you work so that your cottage looks great from all angles.

06 To get really precise edges, use one needle and a straight finger as a guide. Again using just one needle in your holder and working with tiny jabs, smooth and tidy the surface of your little house by needle felting thin layers of fiber to cover the cottage walls and roof.

07 Now take a small amount of white roving and anchor a covering of snow to the roof. Outline the edge first in loose, natural waves, then fill it in. This is best done with one needle for a crisper finish.

08 Needle felt a little door onto the front of your house, and embroider and embellish as you choose. For example, sew on heart-shaped buttons for windows and seed beads to make the snow-covered roof glisten.

09 Finally, stitch a little jump ring into the top of the house, twist some matching embroidery floss into a cord, and thread them through. Tie the ends of the twisted cord to a binder ring ready for hanging.

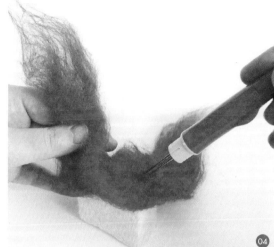

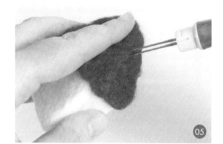

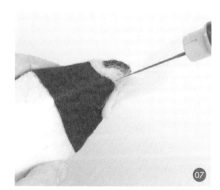

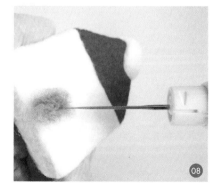

GRETEL PARKER

Children's illustrator Gretel Parker discovered needle felting four years ago. Now her work is collected all over the world and she enjoys passing on her knowledge and spreading the needle felting "bug" to new crafters.
www.gretelparker.com

MIX AND MATCH
HEIRLOOM STOCKING

USE FESTIVE FABRICS, OR TEAM YOUR FAVORITE FLORALS WITH BARGAIN VINTAGE FINDS. FINISH OFF WITH YOUR CHOICE OF RICKRACK, RIBBONS, LACE, AND DOILIES. HANG ABOVE THE FIREPLACE, AND — FINGERS-CROSSED — YOUR STOCKING WILL SOON BE FULL OF GORGEOUS GIFTS.

HOMEMADE DECORATION

HOW TO MAKE ... HEIRLOOM STOCKING

MATERIALS

FABRIC, ABOUT ½ YARD (0.5 METER)
FOR EACH STOCKING

TRIMMINGS: RIBBONS, RICKRACK, LACE,
BUTTONS, DOILIES

SCISSORS

SEWING MACHINE

SEWING NEEDLE

PINS

TIP
For an alternative design, cut a doily in half and shape the toe and heel using templates C and D as a guide. The yo yo flower can be replaced with a simple ribbon trimmed button.

01 Gather together your materials, choosing fabric and trimmings that complement each other. Photocopy the templates, scaling up as necessary, and cut out of paper. Fold your fabric neatly in half, and using template A cut out two stocking shapes from your main fabric.

02 Choose your lining fabric (if different) and cut out two more stocking shapes as in step 1. Using templates B, C and D, cut out one of each shape in your contrasting fabrics for your stocking top, toe and heel.

03 Press a ⅜" (1 cm) hem at the bottom edge of the stocking top. Lay one main stocking piece flat, with right side facing you, and pin the stocking top in place. Machine stitch onto the stocking, and add any ribbons, lace or rickrack, pinning them in place before sewing on.

04 Next take your heel and toe pieces, pin in place, then sew onto the stocking. Use a zigzag stitch for added embellishment.

05 Take both main stocking pieces and pin right sides together. Machine stitch using a ⅜" (1 cm) seam allowance, trim edges and snip into curves to allow for neat turning. Turn right way out and press over a ⅝" (1.5 cm) hem around the top of the stocking.

06 Take the two lining pieces, pin and machine stitch right sides together with a ⅜" (1 cm) seam allowance. Trim and snip seams (as step 5) but do not turn right way out. Press a ⅝" (1.5 cm) hem along the top. Place the lining inside the main stocking.

07 Take a piece of ribbon about 6¼" (16 cm) long, fold in half and place the ends in between the main stocking and stocking lining at the top right of the stocking. Pin in place. Machine stitch a ¼" (6 mm) hem around the top of the stocking and press.

08 To make the yo yo flower, cut a circle of fabric 4" (10 cm) and hand sew a running stitch along the edge all the way round. Draw up to gather the outside edge inward and sew down in the center.

09 Add a button to the center and trim with ribbon. Sew the finished yo yo flower onto the stocking top.

SEE P95
FOR
TEMPLATES

06

01

08

JANE HUGHES

Jane from littleteawagon is a crafter/
designer with a fondness for British
70s fabrics and wallpapers …
making homewares and bags and
blogging about a crafty life.
www.teawagontales.blogspot.com

03

04

09

CROCHET REINDEER

THIS CHRISTMASSY CREATURE MAY OR MAY NOT BE RELATED TO SANTA'S FAVORITE GIFT-DISTRIBUTING REINDEER, BUT HE CERTAINLY SHARES RUDOLPH'S GLOWING RED NOSE! MAKE HIM AS A STOCKING-FILLER PRESENT OR ADD HIM TO YOUR FESTIVE DÉCOR.

HOW TO MAKE ... CROCHET REINDEER

MATERIALS

100ɢ BALLS (306 YARDS/280 METERS) OF HAYFIELD BONUS DK, ONE EACH IN OATMEAL #964 (A), ALPINE #842 (B), AND CHOCOLATE #947 (C), OR SIMILAR YARN (DK-WEIGHT ACRYLIC)

ODDMENTS OF RED AND WHITE DK YARN

CROCHET HOOKS, SIZE C2/D3 (3 ᴍᴍ) AND SIZE E4 (3.5 ᴍᴍ)

90 ᴏᴢ (50 ɢ) POLYESTER TOY STUFFING

105 ᴏᴢ (60 ɢ) POLYPROPYLENE GRANULES

TWO BLACK SEED BEADS FOR EYES

TWO PIPE CLEANERS

SEWING NEEDLE

PINS

GAUGE TIP

Gauge is not important for this project, as long as you make the crochet fabric nice and dense so the various items can be stuffed firmly and retain their shapes.

01 Make the body (starting at tail end). With yarn A and E4 hook, make a magic loop, ch1, and work 6sc into the loop. Sl st to the first ch to join.
Round 1: Ch1, 1sc into each st, sl st to the first ch to join.
Round 2: Ch1, 2sc into each st, sl st to the first ch to join. 12 sts
Round 3: Ch1, (2sc in the first st, 1sc) six times, sl st to the first ch to join. 18 sts
Round 4: Ch1, (2sc in the first st, 2sc) six times, sl st to the first ch to join. 24 sts
Round 5: Ch1, (2sc in the first st, 5sc) four times, sl st to the first ch to join. 28 sts
Work another five rounds of 28sc.
Next round: Ch1, (sc2tog, 2sc) seven times, sl st to the first ch to join. 21 sts
Next round: Ch1, 21sc, sl st to the first ch to join.
Next round: Ch1, (sc2tog, 1sc) seven times, sl st to the first ch to join. 14 sts
Next round: Ch1, 14sc, sl st to the first ch to join.
Fill most of body with granules.
Next round: Ch1, (sc2tog) seven times, sl st to the first ch to join. 7 sts
Next round: Ch1, 7sc, sl st to the first ch to join.

Fasten off, top up the stuffing using polypropylene granules and then sew up the hole.

02 Make the head.
With yarn A and E4 hook, make a magic loop, ch1, and work 6sc into the loop. Sl st to the first ch to join.
Round 1: Ch1, 2sc into each st, sl st to the first ch to join. 12 sts
Round 2: Ch1, (2sc in the first st, 1sc) six times, sl st to the first ch to join. 18 sts
Work another four rounds of 18sc.
Next round: Ch1, (2sc in the first st, 5sc) three times, sl st to the first ch to join. 21 sts
Next round: Ch1, 21sc, sl st to the first ch to join.
Next round: Ch1, (2sc in the first st, 2sc) seven times, sl st to the first ch to join. 28 sts
Change to yarn B.
Next round: Ch1, 28sc, sl st to the first ch to join.
Next round: Rep last round.
Next round: Ch1, (sc2tog, 2sc) seven times, sl st to the first ch to join. 21 sts
Next round: Ch1, (sc2tog, 1sc) seven times, sl st to the first ch to join. 14 sts
Stuff with polyester toy stuffing.

Abbreviations

beg: beginning

ch: chain

cont: continue

magic loop and ch 1: Make a loop with the yarn around your index finger so that there are two strands at the point where the ends pass one another. Put your hook underneath these two strands and pick up the yarn (make sure you use the working end which runs to the skein rather than the tail end), pulling it under the strands so that the yarn is over the hook. Pick up the yarn again and pull it through the loop on the hook to make one chain.

rep: repeat

sc: single crochet

sc2tog: single crochet two stitches together (decrease by one stitch): insert the hook in the first st, yarn round hook and pull it through this stitch (2 loops on hook). Insert the hook into the second st, yarn round hook and pull it through this stitch (3 loops on hook). Yarn round hook and pull through all 3 loops on hook.

sl st: slip(ped) stitch

st(s): stitch(es)

01

TIP
When filling the body with poly-propylene granules, you might find it helpful to use a funnel made from a piece of paper to get them in – otherwise they may easily spill out.

02

Next round: Ch1, (sc2tog) seven times, sl st to the first ch to join. 7 sts
Fasten off, top up the stuffing using polyester toy stuffing and sew up hole, leaving a long tail of yarn to sew the head to the body.

03 Make four legs.
With yarn A and E4 hook, make a magic loop, ch1, and work 6sc into the loop. Cont without closing off the round with a sl st, so the next st to be worked will be the first of the 6sc. Cont working in a spiral in this fashion until the leg measures 1½" (4 cm). Fasten off, leaving a long tail of yarn to sew the legs to the body.
Fold a piece of pipe cleaner double so that it fits inside the length of the leg.

04 Sew the head on securely so that the top of the head is level with the top of the body. Make sure the seam of the head is turned toward the back, and that the seam of the body is underneath.

05 Make two ears.
With yarn A and E4 hook, ch3 and join into a ring with a sl st.
Row 1: Ch1, 3sc into ring, turn.
Row 2: Ch1, 1sc, 2sc in next st, 1sc, turn. 4 sts

Row 3: Ch1, (sc2tog) twice, turn. 2 sts
Row 4: Ch1, sc2tog. 1 st
Fasten off, leaving a tail of yarn to sew the ears to the head.
Pinch the base of each ear together and sew with a couple of stitches before attaching each ear to the top of the head.

06 Make the tail.
With yarn A and E4 hook, ch5.
Row 1: Work 4sc beg with the second ch from the hook, ch1 and 4sc along the other side of foundation ch without turning. Sl st into the point of the tail. Fasten off, leaving a long tail of yarn to sew the tail to the body. Sew in position just above the starting point of the body.

07 Sew the legs in position underneath the body.

08 Make two antlers.
With yarn C and C2/D3 hook, ch7. Leave a long tail of yarn at beg of the chain for sewing the antlers to the head.
Row 1: Work 6sc beg with the second ch from the hook, turn.
Row 2: Sl st across 3 sts beg with the st at the base of the hook, ch7.

Row 3: Work 6sc beg with the second ch from the hook, sl st into the first piece of 6sc to join, turn.
Row 4: Sl st across 3 sts beg with the st at the base of the hook, ch4.
Row 5: Work 3sc beg with the second ch from the hook, sl st into the second piece of 6sc to join, Fasten off.

09 Flip one antler over so that the antlers are symmetrical and sew to the top of the head.

10 Make the nose.
With red yarn and E4 hook, make a magic loop and 6sc into loop. Sl st to the first ch to join and fasten off, leaving a long tail of yarn to sew the nose to the head.

11 Add the finishing touches.
Sew the nose to the head. Mark the position of the eyes with two pins. Sew a few straight stitches with white yarn at these two points, and sew two black seed beads on top.

CARA MEDUS

Cara lives in Bristol U.K. with her husband and two boys. She loves designing things to knit and crochet, and occasionally finds some time to do a bit of illustration and papercraft. Her other passions are cake and coffee, preferably at the same time. www.caramedus.com

LINO-CUT
FESTIVE STATIONERY

IT'S EASIER THAN YOU THINK TO CREATE YOUR OWN LINO-CUT STAMP. YOU WILL SOON BE PRINTING MATCHING CARDS, ENVELOPES, LABELS, WRAPPING PAPER, AND WHATEVER ELSE YOU CAN GET YOUR HANDS ON!

PUT YOUR OWN STAMP ON IT!

merry christmas

HOW TO MAKE ... FESTIVE STATIONERY

MATERIALS

SPEEDY CARVE LINO BLOCK

LINO CUTTER AND BLADE

PENCIL

TRACING PAPER

SELECTION OF COLORED CARD,
PAPER, GIFT TAGS, AND ENVELOPES

INK PADS IN A SELECTION OF COLORS

SCISSORS

SEE P95 FOR TEMPLATES

01 Draw or trace a simple shape on a piece of tracing paper to create your stamp. Use the templates provided. Silhouettes work the best; think about what you would like to print and if you would like the image to be a positive or negative print.

02 Turn the tracing paper over and transfer trace your drawing onto your speedy carve lino block, making sure to leave space for cutting out around each. The pencil line should now be visible on your block.

03 Cut your designs out using scissors. Each will become a stamp.

04 Using the lino cutter very carefully cut away the lino around your design or inside your design depending on whether you would like to create a negative or positive print.

05 Now your lino stamp is complete, use your ink pads to ink it up and then press firmly onto your chosen paper, card, or gift tag to create your print.

TIP
Experiment with papers, colors and repeat printing to create patterns for your stationery.

ZEENA SHAH

Zeena Shah studied printed textile design at the U.K. Chelsea School of Art & Design and has since worked in both the fashion and interiors textile industry. In late 2009, inspired by her love of paper cutting, printing, birds and hearts, she launched her own label, z e e n a – a collection of hand silk-screen printed and handmade textiles for the home. Zeena also runs a program of craft workshops, inspiring people to get stitching.
www.zeenashah.com

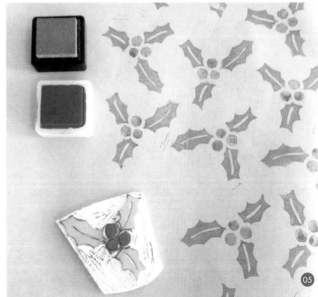

FELT RUFFLE
DOOR WREATH

GIVE THE WELCOMING DOOR WREATH, THAT TRADITIONAL FESTIVE DECORATION, A BRIGHT, MODERN LOOK. THE RUFFLES ARE EASILY MADE FROM FOLDED CIRCLES OF FELT PINNED IN PLACE ON A POLYSTYRENE BASE, AND THEN DECORATED WITH A MACHINE-STITCHED MISTLETOE EMBELLISHMENT. EASY TO MAKE RIBBON BOWS ADD A LUXURIOUS TOUCH.

HOW TO MAKE ... DOOR WREATH

MATERIALS

PURPLE FELT FOR THE WREATH, 1³/₄ YARDS (1.5 METERS) OF 36" (90 CM) WIDE

BRIGHT GREEN FELT, 10 x 10" (25 x 25 CM) PLUS SCRAPS OF WHITE FELT

GREEN SEWING MACHINE THREAD A SHADE DARKER THAN THE FELT

SATIN RIBBON IN GREEN AND PURPLE, 1 YARD (1 METER) EACH OF ³/₄" (2 CM) WIDE

NARROW RIBBON, 3¹/₈" (8 CM), FOR HANGING

DRESSMAKER'S PINS, ABOUT 175

POLYSTYRENE HALF-RING FORM, 10" (25 CM)

SCISSORS

WATER-ERASABLE FABRIC PEN

SEWING MACHINE

TIP
When fixing the ruffles to the polystyrene wreath you may want to use a thimble to press in the pins, especially as there are so many to attach!

01 Cut a 3¹/₈" (8 cm) circle card template and use to mark about 150 circles onto purple felt as close together as possible. Cut out.

02 To make a ruffle, take a felt circle, fold in half and crease to give you a semicircle. Fold in half again and put a pin through the point of the quarter circle.

03 To attach the felt ruffle to the wreath, push in the pin. Continue to fold and add more, arranging them at different angles to enhance the ruffled effect, and grouping them tightly so that the polystyrene cannot be seen.

04 To make the hanging loop, cut a 3¹/₈" (8 cm) length of narrow ribbon. Fold in half and attach it to the back of the wreath with two or three pins.

05 Use the mistletoe template to cut 9 sprigs from green felt. Cut out 36 small berries about ¼" (6 mm) in diameter from white felt.

06 Machine stitch the veins onto the sprigs. Start at the stem and stitch a row of small straight stitches down the center and half way down the lowest leaf. Leaving the needle in

the felt, raise the foot and rotate to stitch back up the leaf and up the stem. Continue to stitch veins down each leaf working your way back up to the top of the stem. As you stitch, the felt should curl slightly to create the mistletoe shape.

07 On each sprig, place a berry where each leaf meets the stem; machine stitch in place. Take three mistletoe sprigs and lay the stems on top of each other; machine stitch in place. Make two more sprig groups.

08 Use pins to attach the sprig groups to the lower half of the wreath in between the ruffles, making sure to press the pins in firmly.

09 To make a bow, take a 1 yard (1 meter) length of ribbon and fold down one end by 4" (10 cm). Continue to fold the ribbon in 4" (10 cm) folds, one on top of the other. Machine a few small stitches at the center to secure and insert two pins where you have stitched.

10 Fold the bow in half pulling all loops up together, then push it into the wreath in between the ruffles, where the mistletoe stems meet. Make and insert a second ribbon bow.

SEE P95
FOR
TEMPLATES

02

03

06

HELEN NEWTON

Passionate about sewing and
crafting, Helen loves to create
beautiful, contemporary items using
simple to learn techniques. Her
aim is to inspire others to make
something unique and original while
having fun along the way.
www.lillyblossom.co.uk
www.etsy.com/lillyblossom

07

08

09

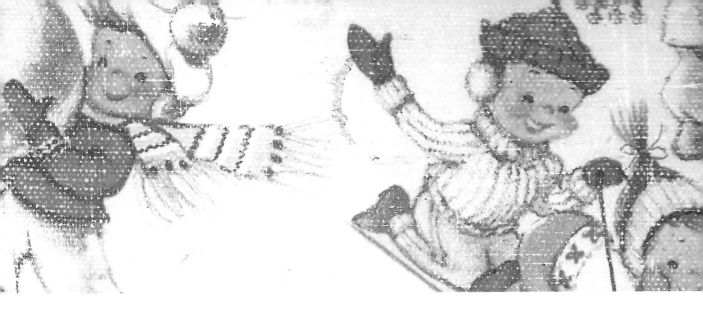

SIMPLE CROCHET
GRANNY SQUARE GARLAND

BRING A LITTLE FESTIVE FUN TO YOUR HOME WITH THIS VIBRANT CROCHET GARLAND.
THIS IS A GREAT STASH-BUSTING PROJECT AS EACH GRANNY SQUARE ONLY REQUIRES
A SMALL AMOUNT OF YARN, AND THE MORE COLORS YOU USE, THE MORE LIVELY
THE EFFECT!

GREAT FOR BEGINNERS

HOW TO MAKE ... GRANNY SQUARE GARLAND

MATERIALS

DK YARNS IN YOUR CHOSEN COLORS

CROCHET HOOK SIZE, E4 (3.5 MM)

SCISSORS

DARNING NEEDLE

GAUGE TIP

Gauge is not important for this project, but using the same type of yarn for each square should ensure that all the squares end up the same size.

01 Make a slipknot in the end of the yarn and put the loop on to the crochet hook, then ch 4. Join with sl st into first ch to form a ring.

02 **Round 1:** 3ch (counts as 1dc), 2dc into ring, 3ch, 3dc into ring, 3ch, *3dc into ring, 3ch, rep from * once more, sl st into top of first ch.

03 **Round 2:** Sl st across next 2dc to reach first corner ch sp, 3ch (counts as 1dc), 2dc into the first corner ch sp, 3ch, 3dc into the same ch sp (makes 1st corner), *3dc into next ch sp, 3ch, 3dc into same ch sp (makes 2nd corner); rep from * to make the 3rd and 4th corners, complete the round with sl st into top of first ch.

04 **Round 3:** Sl st across next 2dc to reach first corner ch sp, 3ch (counts as 1dc), 2dc into the first corner sp, 3ch, 3dc into same ch sp (makes 1st corner), *3dc into next ch sp (ch sp between the two sets of 3dc on the last round), 3dc into second corner sp, 3ch, 3dc into same ch sp (makes 2nd corner); rep from * to make 3rd and 4th corners, 3dc into final ch sp, complete the round with sl st into top of first ch.

05 **Round 4:** Sl st across next 2dc to reach first corner ch sp, 3ch (counts as 1dc), 2dc into first corner sp, 3ch, 3dc into same ch sp (makes 1st corner), *3dc into next ch sp, 3dc into next ch sp, 3dc into second corner sp, 3ch, 3dc into same ch sp (makes 2nd corner); rep from * to complete the 3rd and 4th corners, 3dc into next ch sp, 3dc into final ch sp, complete the round with sl st into top of first ch.

06 Cut yarn and weave in the loose yarn ends with the darning needle. Make 12 granny squares in all.

07 Join the squares together to make a garland. Choose a color for the chain to attach all the squares together and ch 50 to make the garland end.

08 Take your first square and ch into the top edge of the square to attach it, then ch into the top of every st along one edge of the square (should be about 14 or 15ch for each edge to make sure the edge remains nice and square). Make 10ch for the length of garland between the first square and the next square.

09 Repeat step 8 until all 12 squares are attached, then make 50ch for the second garland end and tie off.

TIP
If you prefer a more traditional theme to your Christmas décor, make the squares in forest green and holly-berry red, or use bright whites and metallic yarns for a snowflake effect.

DESIGNED BY JANE HUGHES

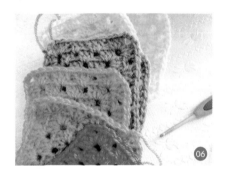

Abbreviations

ch: chain
ch sp: chain space
dc: double crochet
rep: repeat
sl st: slip(ped) stitch

TRIM THE TREE

FESTIVE IDEAS

01

A pretty paper and clothes pin angel design from Kirsty Neale that can be used to clip up Christmas cards, decorate your tree or as a cute alternative to a bow, holding gift tags in place. www.kirstyneale.typepad.com

02

These sweet decorations from Eva Gáti are so simple to make – roll your paper into a cone, trim the excess at the top, edge with lace ribbon and add a handle. Make 24 for a Christmas tree advent calendar. For more great ideas from Eva visit her blog kiflieslevendula.blogspot.com

03

Let Annabelle Ozanne's "Lil branch of glee…" inspire you to transform a tree branch into a Christmas display, adorned with handmade paper and crochet decorations and thrift store purchases. threeredapples.blogspot.co.uk

DECK THE WALLS

04

This little wooden Christmas tree by Ingrid Jansen of Wood & Wool Stool is handmade from recycled pieces of wood with small hooks screwed in to add decorations. A small piece of string is attached to the back so it can be hung on the wall. For more designs see www.woodwoolstool.com

05

If you make your own stocking it can be as large as you like! This design from Charlotte Lyons is made using her Walnut Hill Farm range of patterned material and you can have fun embroidering the details in the fabric. www.blendfabrics.com

06

This bunting-style advent calendar from Jooles Hill, and made from Tilda fabrics, will help you to count down the crafty days to Christmas. For lots more festive ideas visit Joole's blog sewsweetviolet.blogspot.co.uk

SCANDINAVIAN-STYLE
PAPER CUT ORNAMENT

THIS PAIR OF PAPER CUT DECORATIONS ARE BASED ON THE WOODEN DALA HORSES OF SWEDEN. ORIGINALLY MADE AS TOYS FOR CHILDREN, THEY WERE CARVED IN THE LONG, DARK WINTER EVENINGS, THEN PAINTED IN BRIGHTLY COLORED PATTERNS. MAKE YOURS IN RED AND WHITE, THE TRADITIONAL CHRISTMAS COLORS OF SCANDINAVIA.

MAKE A
MATCHING
PAIR

HOW TO MAKE ... PAPER CUT ORNAMENT

MATERIALS

TWO SHEETS OF PAPER, 8½ x 11" (A4) WHITE

TWO SHEETS OF CARDSTOCK, 8½ x 11" (A4) RED

TRACING PAPER

PENCILS, H AND 2H

GLUE

SMALL PAIR OF SHARP, POINTED SCISSORS

CRAFT KNIFE AND RULER

TIP

For a pretty garland, mount a number of paper cut horses on different colored card and attach to lengths of ribbon. Or make miniature versions as place cards for the Christmas table.

01 Use a soft H pencil to trace off the horse design from the template. Turn the tracing paper over, lay it down on a sheet of white paper and use the harder 2H pencil to go over the inner outline of the horse and the marked patterns.

02 Cut out the shape and following the fold lines on the template, fold the horse in half and half again, making sure that the center panel design is on the outside of the fold (see photo).

03 Use a small pair of sharp, pointed scissors to cut away the design.

04 Open up the horse and fold over the tail section along the fold line marked on the template. Cut out the triangle pattern and open out. Repeat for cutting the patterns first on the legs, then the neck, and finally the eye section.

05 Transfer the outer outline of the horse onto some red cardstock and cut out.

06 Cut out two stands from red cardstock and score down the edge of each ⅜" (1 cm) in from the side, following the line marked on the template and using a craft knife to just break the surface. Crease the scored lines to form glue flaps.

07 Glue the white paper cut to the red card – pencil marks facing down – making sure that you have a border of red card all around. If you are using a glue stick, take care on the delicate cut section as it can tear. Alternatively, you could use an adhesive spray: work in a well-ventilated area and follow the manufacturer's instructions.

08 Glue the stands to the back of the horse, lining up the base with the bottom edge of the legs.

09 Repeat steps 1–8 to make another horse, but this time turn the trace over so that the horse faces the other way.

SEE P93 FOR TEMPLATES

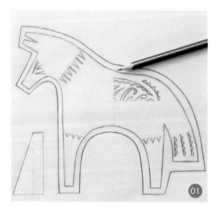

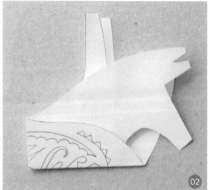

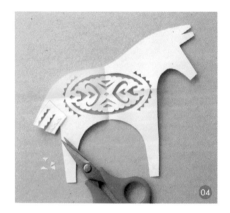

CLARE YOUNGS

Designer-maker Clare was given a craft book with a pile of paper and fabric at the age of eight and she hasn't stopped making since! Having trained as a graphic designer, she worked in packaging and illustration until turning to craft full time five years ago. Clare has written several craft books – to find out more visit www.clare@youngs-studio.com

HAND-EMBROIDERED
BAUBLE GIFT BAGS

SEW UP THESE LITTLE BAGS TO ADD A HANDMADE TOUCH TO SMALL GIFTS AND FESTIVE TREATS. AT JUST 3½" (9 CM) WIDE AND 6½" (16.5 CM) HIGH (INCLUDING HANDLES), THEY ARE SMALL ENOUGH TO HANG FROM THE TREE. THE HARDEST PART OF THIS PROJECT IS CHOOSING WHICH OF THE FIVE SMILING ORNAMENT MOTIFS TO EMBROIDER!

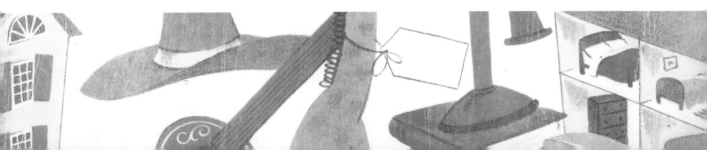

HOW TO MAKE ... BAUBLE GIFT BAGS

SEE P94 FOR TEMPLATES

MATERIALS: PER GIFT BAG

LIGHT-COLORED COTTON FABRIC, 5 x 5"
(13 x 13 cm)

EMBROIDERY FLOSS: SILVER GRAY, BLACK,
AND BRIGHT CHRISTMAS COLOURS

BRIGHTLY COLORED FELT, 4 x 12" (10 x 30 cm)
FOR BAG

CONTRASTING FELT, TWO PIECES ⅜ x 6"
(1 x 15 cm) FOR HANDLES

WATER-ERASABLE FABRIC PEN

EMBROIDERY HOOP AND
EMBROIDERY NEEDLE

SCISSORS, PINS AND IRON

TIP
Made from felt, these little bags
are perfect for lightweight gifts,
but if you do plan to place
something a little heavier in the
bag, double the handles so they
don't stretch.

01 Trace your chosen motif onto the
light-colored fabric. Place the fabric
in the embroidery hoop to keep it
nice and taut as you stitch.

02 Embroider your chosen motif. Use six
strands of floss and stem stitch for the
ornament outline, and three strands
for everything else. Use backstitch
(see p87) for the ornament details,
French knots (see p87) for the eyes,
and an open detached chain for the
mouth.

03 Remove the embroidered fabric
from the hoop and trim to 2¾ x 3½"
(7 x 9 cm).

04 Fold the bag felt in half. Place the
gift bag template on the fold, pin in
place and trim around the sides and
top edge. Cut out the opening on
one side only.

05 Pin the embroidered panel into the
opening. Use running stitch (see p87)
and three strands to sew in place.

06 Stitch each handle in place inside the
scalloped edge using a single cross
stitch using three strands of floss.

07 Fold the bag in half, right sides
facing, and press. Keeping the

crease together, fold the bag back
on itself, wrong sides facing, and
make a ½" (1.3 cm) gusset each
side of the fold. Pin in place.

08 Stitch the sides of the bag with
running stitch and three strands.

09 Make more bags using different
motifs – there are five to choose.

MOLLIE JOHANSON

Mollie Johanson began her blog
Wild Olive as a creative outlet.
Dreaming and doodling have
resulted in embroidery and paper
projects, most featuring simply
expressive faces. Mollie lives near
Chicago, commuting daily to her
in-home studio via the coffee pot.
www.wildolive.blogspot.co.uk

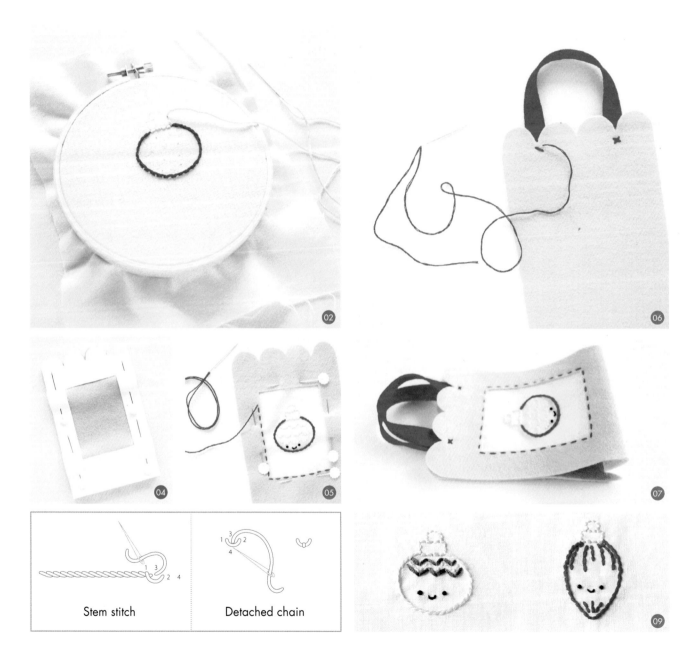

Stem stitch

Detached chain

FELT APPLIQUÉ

IPAD COZY

DRESS UP YOUR FAVORITE GADGET FOR THE HOLIDAY SEASON WITH THIS SUPER SNUG COZY FEATURING A GREAT LITTLE RETRO DEER MOTIF. FELT IS ONE OF THE EASIEST MATERIALS TO WORK WITH AND THIS SIMPLE DESIGN CAN BE COMPLETELY STITCHED BY HAND — NO SEWING MACHINE REQUIRED!

SCALE UP OR DOWN FOR OTHER GADGETS

HOW TO MAKE ... IPAD COZY

MATERIALS

TWO PIECES OF BABY BLUE FELT,
13 x 8¼" (33 x 21 CM)

ONE PIECE EACH OF RED AND BEIGE FELT,
8 x 5" (20 x 13 CM)

SCRAPS OF BABY BLUE, MEDIUM BROWN,
DARK BROWN, PINK, AND WHITE FELT
FOR ACCENTS

EMBROIDERY FLOSS: RED, BLUE, BEIGE, WHITE,
AND BLACK

SIX SMALL OPAQUE SEED BEADS

SMALL PAIR OF SHARP, POINTED SCISSORS

FABRIC GLUE

SHARP SEWING NEEDLE

TIP
Don't have an iPad? No worries!
Just reduce the template sizes to
fit your favorite gadget, or make
it into a heating pad
cover instead.

01 Use the templates to cut out the following pieces from your felt fabric: a red oval, beige deer, medium brown ear details, white eye, blue collar, and three pink baubles. You will also need a small circle of dark brown felt for the deer's pupil and a slightly larger circle of dark brown felt for his nose.

02 Take one of your baby blue felt rectangles and pin the red felt oval onto it 2" (5 cm) from the bottom. Hand sew securely in place with small neat running stitches, using a sharp needle and a single strand of red embroidery floss.

03 Pin the deer motif on top of the red oval and hand stitch in place, again with running stitch, using a single strand of beige embroidery floss to match your felt color.

04 Glue or stitch on the smaller felt accents using the photograph on p43 as your guide. When you are happy that all the felt layers are securely in place, use a sharp needle and single strand of black embroidery floss to add the eyelashes to the eye and long stitches to the hanging baubles.

05 To finish the embellishment of the front of the iPad cozy, add a few freehand snowflakes in opposite corners of the design using a single strand of white embroidery floss and the opaque seed beads. Our design has a total of six, but you can add as many as you like for a more festive finish.

06 Before stitching together the back and front pieces of your iPad cozy, you need to strengthen the top edges of the felt. Simply fold over the top edge of each piece by 2" (5 cm) towards the right side of the fabric. Using blue embroidery floss, secure each flap by stitching down the sides and along the bottom edge with a neat running stitch.

07 Align the front and the back pieces of your iPad cozy, wrong sides together, and pin in place. With the deer motif facing you, blanket stitch all the way around the edges using all six strands of blue embroidery floss to match.

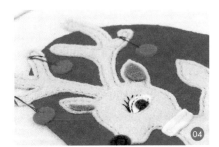

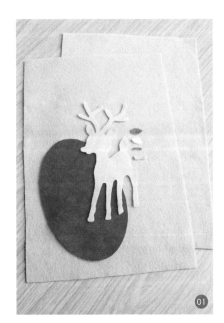

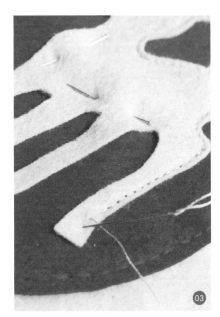

SEE P95 FOR TEMPLATES

CHARLIE MOORBY
aka THE SAVVY CRAFTER

Charlie is a thrifty craft blogger and incurable stitching addict with a penchant for anything handmade. Commissioning Editor by day and crafter by night you'll find her collecting buttons and hoarding ribbons on a daily basis.
She's a dab hand with a pencil and loves a bit of cross stitching too.
Find her online at
thesavvycrafter.blogspot.co.uk

BABY BOOTIES

ADD A TOUCH OF SPARKLE TO BABY'S FIRST CHRISTMAS WITH THESE CUTE BEADED BOOTEES. WITH A CLASSIC T-BAR BUTTON STRAP, THEY FIT SNUGLY AND SECURELY AROUND BABY'S FEET. THE INSTRUCTIONS PROVIDED ARE FOR THE CREAM BOOTIES WITH RED SOLES BUT, AS YOU CAN SEE, YOU CAN EASILY CHANGE THE COLOR OF THE YARN AND BEADS.

HOW TO MAKE ... BABY BOOTIES

MATERIALS: CREAM BOOTIES

50ɢ BALLS (93 YARDS/80 METERS) OF ROWAN HANDKNIT COTTON, ONE EACH IN ECRU #251 (A), AND ROSSO #215 (B), OR SIMILAR YARN (DK-WEIGHT COTTON)

KNITTING NEEDLES, ONE PAIR OF SIZE 3 (3.25 MM)

DEBBIE ABRAHAMS SEED BEADS SIZE 6/0: ONE PACKET OF CLEAR BEADS

SHARP SEWING NEEDLE AND FINE SEWING THREAD TO STRING THE BEADS ONTO YARN

TAPESTRY NEEDLE

TWO SMALL SHELL BUTTONS

GAUGE TIP

25 sts and 32 rows to 4" (10 cm) square over St st using size 3 needles. Finished size approx 3½" (9 cm) long; width at toe about 1¾" (4.5 cm).

01 Thread the beads onto your main colour yarn (yarn A) before you start the pattern. You will need about 76 beads per bootie, but it is best to string more beads than are required than too few. Take a 4" (10 cm) length of sewing cotton and thread a sharp sewing needle with it. Tie a knot at the end to form a loop. Place the end of the yarn through the sewing thread loop and press the fold of yarn with your finger and thumb to flatten slightly; this will help the beads to slide on more easily. Next, pick up a bead with the sewing needle, slip the bead down the needle and thread, and then slip it down onto the yarn. Repeat this process until all 76 beads have been threaded onto the yarn.

02 Knit the cream booties (make 2 the same).
Start with the sole:
Using yarn B and size 3 needles, cast on 30 sts.
Row 1: K1, yo, k13, yo, k1, yo, k1, yo, k13, yo, k1. 35 sts
Row 2: K1, ktbl, k13, ktbl, k1, ktbl, k1, ktbl, k13, ktbl, k1.
Row 3: K2, yo, k13, yo, k2, yo, k3, yo, k13, yo, k2. 40 sts
Row 4: K2, ktbl, k13, ktbl, k3, ktbl, k2, ktbl, k13, ktbl, k2.

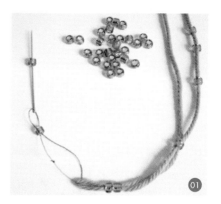

CAROL MELDRUM

Carol is a textile designer, author and workshop tutor based in Glasgow U.K. who enjoys nothing better than playing around with yarn, coming up with new ideas and sharing them with folks at www.beatknit.com and blog.beatknit.com

Row 5: K3, yo, k13, yo, k4, yo, k4, yo, k13, yo, k3. 45 sts
Row 6: K3, ktbl, k13, ktbl, k4, ktbl, k4, ktbl, k13, ktbl, k3.
Break off yarn B.
Join in yarn A.

03 Place beads.
Row 1: K1, *B1, k1, rep from * to end.
Row 2: Purl to end.
Row 3: K2, *B1, k1, rep from * to last st, k1.
Row 4: Purl to end.
Start to shape toe on next row, keeping bead pattern correct.
Row 5: K1, *B1, k1, rep from * until 26 sts have been worked, k2togtbl, turn.
Next row: Sl1, p7, p2tog, turn.
Next row: Sl1, k1, (B1, k1) 3 times, k2togtbl, turn.
Next row: Sl1, p7, p2tog, turn.
Next row: Sl1, (B1, k1) 3 times, B1, k2togtbl, turn.
Next row: Sl1, p7, p2tog, turn.
Next row: Sl1, k1, (B1, k1) 3 times, k2togtbl, turn.
Next row: Sl1, p7, p2tog, turn. 37 sts
Next row: Sl1, k1, *B1, k1, rep from * to end.
Next row: Purl to end.

04 Make top and T-bar.
Now work 3 rows in purl, ending with a RS row.
Bind off 17 sts knitwise, k2 (3 sts on RHN for vertical part of T-bar), bind

off knitwise to end.
Break off yarn.
With RS facing, slip the knitting needle out of the 3 sts and insert back into position as if to work a knit row.
Rejoin yarn and work in garter stitch for 18 rows. Bind off knitwise.

05 Complete strap for left bootie.
With RS facing, and the toe of the bootie to the right, count along 16 sts from the back open edge, insert needle and pick up 3 sts, turn and work 16 rows in garter stitch.
Make buttonhole as follows:
K1, yo, k2togtbl, turn, work a further 2 rows in knit, k3tog, break off yarn.

06 Complete strap for right bootie.
With RS facing, and the toe of the bootie to the left, count along 13 sts from the back open edge, insert needle and pick up 3 sts, turn and work 16 rows in garter stitch.
Make buttonhole as follows:
K1, yfwd, k2togtbl, turn, work a further 2 rows in knit, k3tog, break off yarn.

07 To finish off, sew in all the loose ends, then gently press the toe and sides on the WS of the bootie.
Using mattress stitch, sew up the back seam and sole of the bootie.
To complete the strap, fold over the vertical strap at the front of the bootie towards the inside and sew together to form a loop about

¾" (2 cm) for the horizontal strap to fit through. Slip the horizontal strap through the loop, then sew a button onto the side of the bootie to match up with the buttonhole.

Abbreviations

B1: Bead 1 as follows: bring bead up to back of knitting, bring yarn forward to the front of work between needles, make sure bead is sitting at the front of work, slip the next stitch purlwise, then bring the yarn between the needles to the back of the work, wrapping the slipped stitch and making sure the bead is sitting to the front.
k: knit
k2togtbl: knit two stitches together through the back loop
k3tog: knit three stitches together
ktbl: knit through the back loop
p: purl
p2tog: purl two stitches together
rep: repeat, repeating
RHN: right-hand needle
RS: right side
sl1: slip one stitch
st(s): stitch(es)
St st: stockinette stitch
WS: wrong side
yo: yarnover (between 3 knit stitches)

CROCHET TRADITIONS
SANTA KIT

SANTA HAS TO WORK HARD AT CHRISTMAS TIME, SO IT'S ONLY GOOD MANNERS
TO LEAVE HIM A LITTLE SOMETHING TO SAY THANK YOU. MAKE A BOTTLE AND
A MINCE PIE TO LEAVE BY THE FIRESIDE, AND DON'T FORGET TO MAKE CARROTS
FOR HIS FAITHFUL REINDEER ...

LEAVE OUT
FOR SANTA
EACH YEAR

HOW TO MAKE ... SANTA KIT

MATERIALS: MINCE PIE

100g BALLS (306 YARDS/280 METERS) OF HAYFIELD BONUS DK, ONE EACH IN ALPINE #842 (A) AND CHOCOLATE #947 (B), OR SIMILAR YARN (DK-WEIGHT ACRYLIC)

25g BALLS (77 YARDS/70 METERS) OF HAYFIELD BONUS TOYTIME DK, ONE EACH IN WHITE #961 (C), SIGNAL RED #977 (D) AND EMERALD #916 (E), OR SIMILAR YARN (DK-WEIGHT ACRYLIC)

CROCHET HOOKS, SIZE C2/D3 (3 mm) AND SIZE E4 (3.5 mm)

35 oz (20 g) POLYESTER TOY STUFFING

CARDBOARD

GLUE

SEWING NEEDLE

GAUGE TIP
Gauge is not important for this project, as long as you make the crochet fabric nice and dense so the various items can be stuffed firmly and retain their shapes.

HOW TO MAKE ... THE MINCE PIE

01 Make the pie base.
Using E4 hook and yarn A, make a magic loop, ch1 and 6sc into the loop. Sl st to the first ch to join before pulling up the loop.
Round 1: Ch1, 2sc in each sc of the last round, sl st to the first ch to join. 12 sts
Round 2: Ch1, (2sc in next st, 1sc) six times, sl st to the first ch to join. 18 sts
Round 3: Ch1, (2sc in next st, 2sc) six times, sl st to the first ch to join. 24 sts
Round 4: Ch1, (2sc in next st, 3sc) six times, sl st to the first ch to join. 30 sts
Round 5: Ch1, (2sc in next st, 4sc) six times, sl st to the first ch to join. 36 sts
Round 6: Ch1, 36sc worked in the back loop only, sl st to the first ch to join.
Work another three rounds of 36sc, working through both loops as normal.

02 Make the picot edging.
Next round: Ch1, *sc in next st, ch2, sl st in the first of those ch2, sc in next st **. Rep from * to ** until every st in the round is worked, then sl st to the first ch to join.
Fasten off.

03 Make the mincemeat topping.
Using E4 hook and yarn B, make a magic loop, ch1 and 6sc into the loop. Sl st to the first ch to join before pulling up the loop.
Work rounds 1–5 as for Pie Base.
Work another round of 36sc.
Fasten off.

04 Make the icing.
Using C2/D3 hook and yarn C, make a magic loop, ch1 and 6sc into the loop. Sl st to the first ch to join before pulling up the loop.
Work rounds 1–3 as for Pie Base.
Next row: Ch1, 3sc, turn.
Next row: Ch1, sc2tog, 1sc, turn. 2 sts
Next row: Ch1, sc2tog. 1 st
Sl st down the side of these short rows toward the original round, finishing with a sl st in the st on the end of the first short row. Sl st over the next 2 sts.
Next row: Ch1, 6sc, turn.
Next row: Ch1, sc2tog, 2sc, sc2tog, turn. 4 sts
Next row: Ch1, 1sc, sc2tog, 1sc, turn. 3 sts
Next row: Ch1, sc2tog, 1sc, turn. 2 sts
Next round: Ch1, sc2tog. 1 st

FOR PATTERN ABBREVIATIONS SEE P57

Sl st down the side of these short rows toward the original round, finishing with a sl st in the st on the end of the first short row. Sl st over the next 3 sts.

Next row: Ch1, 4sc, turn.

Next row: Ch1, (sc2tog) twice, turn. 2 sts

Next row: Ch1, sc2tog. 1 st

Sl st down the side of these short rows toward the original round, finishing with a sl st in the st on the end of the first short row. Sl st over the next 2 sts.

Next row: Ch1, 2sc, turn.

Next row: Ch1, 2sc, turn.

Next row: Ch1, sc2tog. 1 st

Sl st down the side of these short rows toward the original round, finishing with a sl st in the st on the end of the first short row.

Sl st over each remaining st to complete the round and sl st to the first ch to join. Fasten off.

05 Make two holly berries.
Using C2/D3 hook and yarn D, make a magic loop, ch1 and 6sc into the loop. Sl st to the first ch to join before pulling up the loop. Fasten off, leaving a long tail of yarn to sew the 6sc together into a small

ball. Use the other end of the yarn to stuff the berry before sewing up.

06 Make two holly leaves.
Using C2/D3 hook and yarn E, ch6. Skip ch at base of hook and sl st in the next ch.
Ch1, *sc in next, ch3, sl st in the first of those ch, sc in next st. **
Rep from * to **.
Ch2 and sl st in the other side of the sc just worked.
Cont working down other side of foundation ch.
Rep from * to ** twice, sl st in the point of the leaf. Fasten off.

07 Make up the mince pie.
Weave in all loose ends. Cut a circular piece of cardboard to fit inside the bottom of the pie base and glue in place.

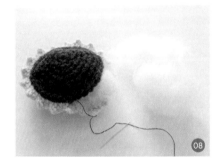

08 Sew the mincemeat topping to the pie base just below the picot edging. Sew nearly all the way round and stuff with polyester toy stuffing before completing the round of sewing.

09 Sew the icing, holly and berries on top of the mince pie.

MATERIALS: BOTTLE

100G BALLS (306 YARDS/280 METERS) OF HAYFIELD BONUS DK, ONE EACH IN CLARET #841 (F) AND ALPINE #842 (A), OR SIMILAR YARN (DK-WEIGHT ACRYLIC)

25G BALLS (77 YARDS/70 METERS) OF HAYFIELD BONUS TOYTIME DK, ONE EACH IN WHITE #961 (C), SIGNAL RED #977 (D), AND BLACK #965 (G), OR SIMILAR YARN (DK-WEIGHT ACRYLIC)

CROCHET HOOKS, SIZE C2/D3 (3 MM) AND SIZE E4 (3.5 MM)

CARDBOARD

GLUE

OLD PAIR OF PANTYHOSE OR A SOCK

105 OZ (60 G) POLYPROPYLENE GRANULES

90 OZ (50 G) POLYESTER TOY STUFFING

TWO BLACK SEED BEADS FOR EYES

GOLD LUREX THREAD

SEWING NEEDLE

THREAD MARKER

HOW TO MAKE ... THE BOTTLE

01 Make the bottle.
Using E4 hook and yarn F, make a magic loop, ch1 and 6sc into the loop. Leave a long tail of yarn from the magic loop (about 12"/30 cm). Sl st to the first ch to join before pulling up the loop.
Work rounds 1–6 as for the Pie Base. Cont to work rounds of 36sc (through both loops of the sc), working in a spiral without closing off the round with a sl st, until the bottle is 3½" (9 cm) high.

02 Weight and stuff the bottle.
Cut a circular piece of cardboard to fit inside the bottom of the bottle. Pierce a hole in the center of the card, and thread the tail of yarn from the magic loop onto a needle and pass it through the hole in the card. Glue the underside of the card to the base of the bottle, and leave the tail of yarn with needle attached. Take the foot from an old pair of pantyhose or sock, and fill it with polypropylene granules so that it makes a small ball that will fit inside the bottle. Tie or sew together the end of the pantyhose/sock, and using the tail of yarn and needle, pass the needle up through the ball

and back down again, through the hole in the piece of card and secure the end to the base of the bottle.

03 Continue working on the bottle.
Place a short piece of thread (use a contrasting color so it is easy to see) between the stitches to mark the beginning of the round, and continue to work in a spiral without closing off the round with a sl st.
Next round: (1sc, sc2tog) twelve times to end of round. 24 sts
Move thread marker up one row after the end of each round.
Next round: (2sc, sc2tog) six times to end of round. 18 sts
Next round: (7sc, sc2tog) twice to the end of round. 16 sts
Next round: (6sc, sc2tog) twice to the end of round. 14 sts
Stuff the bottom portion of the bottle firmly using polyester toy stuffing. You can remove the thread marker.
Cont working in a spiral of sc on these 14 sts until the bottle neck is 2" (5 cm) high.
Change to yarn G, sl st into the next st, ch1, and cont with three rounds of 14sc in black. Sl st to the next st. Stuff neck of bottle using polyester toy stuffing.

Next round: Ch1, (sc2tog) seven times, working in the back loop of the sc only. 7 sts
Sl st to the first ch to join, fasten off and sew up hole.

04 Make the label.
With E4 hook and yarn A, ch13, turn.
Row 1: Work 12sc beg in second ch from hook, turn.
Cont to work another thirteen rows of sc, then fasten off.

05 Make Santa's beard and hair.
With C2/D3 hook and yarn C, ch10, turn.
Row 1: Beg in second ch from hook, 2 sl st, ch1, 1sc in next ch, ch3, skip 3ch, sc in next ch, turn.
Row 2: Ch1, sc2tog (insert hook into ch sp for 2nd of these),1sc into ch sp, sc2tog (insert hook into ch sp for first of these), turn.
Row 3: Ch1, 3sc, 2 sl st down side of beard and 2 sl st in the remaining ch at the end of beard.
Ch10 (to make a line of "hair" that will be sewn along the bottom edge of the hat) and sl st to the other side of the beard to join.
Fasten off.

06 Make Santa's hat.
With C2/D3 hook and yarn D, ch7.
Row 1: Make 6sc beg in second ch from hook, turn.
Row 2: Ch1, sc2tog, 4sc, turn. 5 sts
Row 3: Ch1, 3sc, sc2tog, turn. 4 sts
Row 4: Skip st at base of hook and 3 sl st.
Sl st in the end of each row to carry yarn to the bottom of the hat.
Ch4, skip first ch and 3 sl st back along ch. Sl st to corner of hat to join.
Fasten off.
To make the hat's bobble, work as for holly berry using yarn C.

07 Make up the bottle.
Weave in all loose ends. Sew Santa's "hair" along the edge of the hat. Sew the beard, hair, and hat to the center of the label. Sew the bobble on the end of the hat, and sew two black seed beads for eyes. Make a ch with C2/D3 hook and yarn G long enough to fit just inside the edge of the label and sew in position. Sew the label to the bottle. With gold lurex thread, make a line of chain stitches just inside the edge of the bottle cap.

MATERIALS: CARROT

ONE 100g BALL (494 YARDS/452 METERS) OF SIRDAR COUNTRY STYLE 4PLY, IN CLEMENTINE #541 (H), OR SIMILAR YARN (4PLY-WEIGHT ACRYLIC AND WOOL BLEND)

(OPTIONAL COLOURS FOR MAKING TWO ADDITIONAL CARROTS: TWO SKEINS (9 YARDS/8 METERS) OF DMC TAPESTRY YARN, EACH OF #7947 (I) AND #7052 (J), OR SIMILAR YARN – 4PLY-WEIGHT WOOL)

ONE 25g (77 YARDS/70 METERS) BALL OF HAYFIELD BONUS TOYTIME DK, IN EMERALD #916 (E)

CROCHET HOOK, SIZE E4 (3.5 MM)

35 oz (20 g) POLYESTER TOY STUFFING

SEWING NEEDLE

HOW TO MAKE ... THE CARROT

01 Make carrot for Rudolph.
With E4 hook and yarn H, ch6 and sl st to join into a ring.
Round 1: Ch1, 8sc into the ring, sl st to the ch at beg of round to join.
Round 2: Ch1, 2sc in each sc of last round, sl st to ch at beg of round to join. 16 sts
Cont working 1sc in each st in a spiral, without closing off each round with a sl st, as follows:
Ch1, 48sc (three rounds on these 16 sts).
Sc2tog, 29sc, (counts as two rounds of 15 sts where the sc2tog is 1 st).
Sc2tog, 27sc, (counts as two rounds of 14 sts where the sc2tog is 1 st).
Sc2tog, 25sc, (counts as two rounds of 13 sts where the sc2tog is 1 st).
Cont in this fashion until you have worked:
Sc2tog, 17sc.

Skip 1 st, 8sc.
Skip 1 st, 7sc.
Skip 1 st, 6sc.
Skip 1 st, 5sc.
Skip 1 st, sc2tog, break yarn and fasten off leaving long end and use to sew up end of carrot.

02 Stuff with polyester toy stuffing using the blunt end of the crochet hook to poke stuffing through the hole at the top of the carrot.

03 Optional step: Make carrots for Dancer and Dasher.
If you want to make more carrots for Santa's other little helpers, work as for Rudolph's carrot using yarns I and J.

04 Make up carrot.

Weave in all loose ends. Wind yarn E five or six times around two fingers, and pull these loops off the fingers, holding them together at one end. Use the working end of the yarn to bind these loops together tightly at one end by winding it round several times. Hold this in position firmly and cut the working end of the yarn, leaving about 8" (20 cm) to use for sewing. Thread this end with a needle and sew a couple of stitches through the binding of the loops to secure them. Place the bound end of the loops inside the hole at the top of the stuffed carrot so that the binding is hidden. Sew around the base of the stalk with the tail end of yarn to attach it to the inside of the hole at the top of the carrot. Fasten off. Cut through the loops of the stalk to make individual strands of yarn.

Abbreviations

beg: beginning

ch: chain

ch sp: chain space

cont: continue

magic loop and ch 1: Make a loop with the yarn around your index finger so that there are two strands at the point where the ends pass one another. Put your hook underneath these two strands and pick up the yarn (make sure you use the working end that runs to the skein rather than the tail end), pulling it under the strands so that the yarn is over the hook. Pick up the yarn again and pull it through the loop on the hook to make one chain.

rep: repeat

sc: single crochet

sc2tog: single crochet two stitches together (decrease by one stitch): insert the hook in the first st, yarn round hook and pull it through this stitch (2 loops on hook). Insert the hook into the second st, yarn round hook and pull it through this stitch (3 loops on hook). Yarn round hook and pull through all 3 loops on hook.

sl st: slip(ped) stitch

st(s): stitch(es)

FUN-TO-CUSTOMIZE
SHOPPING TOTE

DECORATE THE FRONT OF A PLAIN, STORE-BOUGHT TOTE BAG WITH THIS SMARTLY DRESSED SANTA. MADE FROM FABRIC AND FELT SCRAPS, HE IS SIMPLE TO SEW. A CONTRAST LINING MAKES THE BAG REVERSIBLE SO YOU CAN USE IT ALL YEAR ROUND AND NOT JUST FOR CHRISTMAS!

GO HO, HO, HO-LIDAY SHOPPING!

HOW TO MAKE ... SHOPPING TOTE

SEE P93 FOR TEMPLATES

MATERIALS

PLAIN CANVAS SHOPPING BAG

SELECTION OF SMALL PIECES OF RED PATTERNED FABRICS

FELT: BLACK, WHITE, AND DARK GRAY

FUSIBLE WEBBING

LIGHTWEIGHT PATTERNED FABRIC FOR THE BAG LINING

EMBROIDERY FLOSS: RED, WHITE, BLACK, PALE PINK, AND DARK GRAY

EMBELLISHMENTS: MINI METAL BUCKLE, TWO RED BUTTONS AND ONE SMALL WHITE POMPOM

SEWING THREADS TO MATCH FELT AND FABRIC COLORS

TRACING PAPER, PENCIL AND WATER-ERASABLE FABRIC PEN

EMBROIDERY AND SEWING NEEDLES

SCISSORS

IRON

SEWING MACHINE (OPTIONAL)

01 Copy the Santa template onto tracing paper, re-sizing it to fit the front of your bag as necessary. Slip the paper template inside the bag and trace it onto the fabric using the water-erasable fabric pen.

02 Take the template out and turn it over to the wrong side. Trace the hat, hat trim, body, belt, legs, boots, gloves, beard, and mustache pieces onto fusible webbing. Iron each piece onto fabric or felt. Cut out as follows: from your selection of red patterned fabrics – hat, body and arms, and legs; from white felt – hat trim, beard, and mustache; from dark gray felt – gloves and boots; from black felt – belt.

03 Peel the paper backing off each piece and arrange on the front of your bag over the relevant part of the traced outline (before placing the belt be sure to thread on the buckle). Iron into place, then stitch around the edges to secure.

04 Sew two buttons to Santa's body and a pompom bobble to his hat. Stitch over the outlines for the facial details to finish the embellishment as follows. Backstitch the nose, mouth, and eyes with dark gray embroidery

floss, adding long stitches for the pupils. Backstitch the cheeks with pink embroidery floss; and work French knots with white floss as close together as possible for the eyebrows.

05 To make the bag lining, fold your patterned lining fabric in half. Place the bag on top, aligning the bottom edge with the fold in the lining fabric. Trim the top and side edges of the lining fabric, leaving a ⅝–¾" (1.5–2 cm) seam allowance all the way around.

06 With right sides facing, stitch along each side edge to join the two layers of fabric together. Press the seams open, then fold over a hem at the top edge (front and back).

07 Place the bag lining inside your embellished bag, making sure to line up the bottom and side edges. Pin the upper hem into place just below the top edge of the bag, then slip stitch to hold the lining in place.

KIRSTY NEALE

Kirsty is a freelance writer and designer-maker. She specializes in fabric and paper projects and enjoys combining new materials with vintage or re-purposed finds. Her work has been published in numerous books and magazines, and she blogs at www.kirstyneale.typepad.com

PAPER FOLD
CHRISTMAS TREE

EVEN THE SMALLEST OF DWELLINGS REQUIRES A CHRISTMAS TREE. THIS ONE IS MADE FROM PRETTY JAPANESE PAPERS IN GREEN, SILVER, AND GOLD AND IS VERY STRAIGHTFORWARD TO MAKE BASED ON A SIMPLE FOLDED FAN SHAPE. YOU COULD JUST AS EASILY MAKE YOURS FROM GIFTWRAP, OR GO FOR AN ALL WHITE LOOK FOR SOPHISTICATED ELEGANCE.

EYE-CATCHING
TABLE
CENTREPIECE

HOW TO MAKE ... CHRISTMAS TREE

DESIGNED BY CLARE YOUNGS

MATERIALS

FOURTEEN PAPER RECTANGLES, TWO OF EACH
8¼ x 11" (21 x 28 CM), 7 x 11" (18 x 28 CM),
6¼ x 11" (16 x 28 CM), 5¼ x 10⅛"
(13.5 x 26 CM), 4¾ x 10⅛" (12 x 26 CM),
3½ x 9⅞" (9 x 25 CM), 2⅜ x 8⅝" (6 x 22 CM)

PATTERNED PAPER FOR THE TRUNK,
4½ x 4½" (11.5 x 11.5 CM)

ONE SHEET OF SILVER PAPER FOR THE BASE,
8½ x 11" (A4)

TWO WOODEN BARBEQUE SKEWERS,
12" (30 CM)

THIN WIRE

PENCIL AND RULER

CRAFT KNIFE AND CUTTING MAT

SMALL PAIR OF SCISSORS

GLUE STICK AND QUICK-DRYING GLUE TUBE

DARNING NEEDLE

01 Start by making the base for the tree. Cut strips of paper ¾" (2 cm) wide. Take the first strip, run a glue stick along one side and start winding it up into a tight coil. As you come to the end of one strip, glue on another strip and continue winding until you have a disc at least 1⅜" (3.5 cm) wide. The wider the base the more stable the tree will be. To ensure your tree stands straight, make the base as flat as possible.

02 Taking one of the larger paper rectangles, place it pattern side down with one of the short edges facing you and fold over by ⅝" (1.5 cm). Turn the paper over and fold the other way, again by ⅝" (1.5 cm). Continue to concertina fold in this way to the end of the strip (if you are left with a spare bit that is not big enough to fold, trim it off).

03 Trim the ends of the folded strip to a point, curving the cut slightly to give a scalloped point.

04 Fold the pleated strip in half and press firmly at the crease. Run a glue stick along one edge of the fan shape and stick to the other edge to make a semicircle.

05 Fold the correspondingly sized paper rectangle in the same way, then stick the two semicircles together to form a complete circle.

06 Take a small piece of wire about 5½" (14 cm) long. Fold it in half and poke the ends through at the center of the circle from front to back on either side of the two joined semicircles. Turn over and twist the ends of the wire together to secure. This completes a branch layer. Repeat steps 2–6 to make the other six branch layers from the pairs of paper rectangles.

07 Take the patterned paper square (for the trunk) and run the glue stick over the reverse side leaving a ¾" (2 cm) strip unglued along one edge. Starting at the unglued edge, roll up to make a tube about ⅝" (1.5 cm) in diameter. Cut into sections as follows: one measuring 1" (2.5 cm), three measuring ¾" (2 cm), and two measuring ⅝" (1.5 cm).

08 Starting with the second smallest circle, begin to thread the paper fold circles onto the skewers, placing the skewer ends through the holes where the wire joins the two semicircles. Setting aside the two smallest paper tubes, use the paper tubes in ascending size to separate the paper fold circles. Push the circles/tubes along the length of the skewers to about ⅝" (1.5 cm) from the top.

09 Once the largest circle has been threaded on, it is time to secure the tree to the base. Prepare the base by using the darning needle to pierce two holes about ⅜" (1 cm) apart either side of the center. Thread on one of the set-aside small paper tubes, place a blob of quick-drying glue into each hole, and push the skewers right down into the holes.

10 Thread the other small paper tube onto the skewers at the top of the tree, place a blob of quick-drying glue onto the end of each skewer and stick the smallest paper fold circle on to finish.

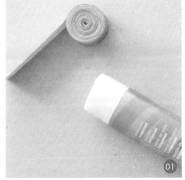

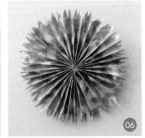

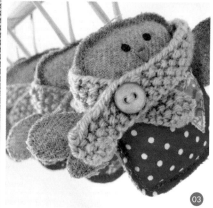

SNOW FLAKES

CHRISTMAS INSPIRATIONS

01

Welcome your Christmas guests with this lovely wreath design from Charlotte Lyons. Wrap a polystyrene form in color co-ordinating scraps, tuck a few decorative trimmings into the folds, and fashion a little bird from felt for the center.
www.charlotte.lyons.com

02

This pretty little snowflake design is just one of six available from Polka & Bloom. Stitch them on table linens or simply leave the fabric in the embroidery hoop and add a festive ribbon for a lovely Christmas ornament.
For the full range of designs see www.polkaandbloom.com and to find out more about their talented designer Carina, visit her blog at carinascraftblog.wardi.dk

03

A flock of Christmas robins, each sporting a sweet little moss stitch scarf, designed by Jooles Hill.
sewsweetviolet.blogspot.co.uk

04

Large snowflake-style plates make lovely candle holders for the Christmas table. Designer Ilaria Chiaratti impressed vintage lace doilies into white modeling clay using a plate as her mould. For more great ideas from Ilaria visit her blog idainteriorlifestyle.blogspot.com

05

Bring a warm glow to your home with this great idea from Eva Gáti. Tealights are displayed in recycled shallow cans decorated with berry-red papers, and hung from a wooden hanger with decorated clothes pins. kiflieslevendula.blogspot.com

06

Why just wrap and tape when you can go 3D? A glue gun takes wrapping to a whole new level, and you can't fail to be inspired by Agnes Blum's extreme gift wrapping ideas.

07

Agnes Blum believes that wrapping makes the present and she shares her top five tips for decorating gifts with you at her blog knockknockingblog.blogspot.co.uk

GIFTWRAP AND CANDLELIGHT

POLAR PALS

FINGER PUPPETS

INSPIRED BY THE INHABITANTS OF THE NORTH AND SOUTH POLES, THESE LITTLE FELT PUPPETS MAKE FANTASTIC CHRISTMAS PRESENTS FOR KIDS. THERE ARE FIVE TO CHOOSE FROM, BUT IF YOU CAN'T BEAR TO GIVE THEM AWAY, STUFF THEM WITH COTTON BALLS TO MAKE SEASONAL DECORATIONS, AND KEEP THEM FOR YOURSELF.

SET OF
FIVE ADORABLE
CHARACTERS

HOW TO MAKE ... FINGER PUPPETS

MATERIALS

FELT: SMALL PIECES OF LIGHT GRAY, DARK GRAY, WHITE, CREAM, BLACK, TEAL, MOSS GREEN, LIGHT BROWN, DARK BROWN, RED, YELLOW, DARK PINK, AND LIGHT PINK

EMBROIDERY FLOSS: BLACK, WHITE, CREAM, DARK GRAY, LIGHT GRAY, LIGHT BROWN, AND TEAL

SMALL SCRAP OF JERSEY FABRIC FOR INUIT GIRL'S SCARF

SMALL BLACK BEADS FOR EYES

SCISSORS

WATER-ERASABLE FABRIC PEN AND TAILOR'S CHALK

PVA OR FABRIC GLUE AND PAINTBRUSH

EMBROIDERY NEEDLE

PINS

TIP
Choose wool felt or a wool fiber blend for best results. Mark your template pieces onto the felt using a water-erasable fabric pen for the lighter colors and tailor's chalk for the darker.

01 To make the snow fox, use the templates and a fabric pen to mark then cut out the required pieces from felt as follows. From gray felt cut one upper head, one tail, and two body pieces. From white felt cut one lower head, one stomach, and one tail tip. Also cut two shallow semicircles from light pink felt for cheeks and a small black felt circle for the nose.

02 Glue the stomach onto one of the body pieces and the tip onto the tail. Stick the upper head onto the lower head, then add one cheek to each side of the lower head, and the nose on the center tip of the upper head.

03 Mark on the eyes and stitch with a single strand of black floss.

04 To create the "fur", sew short, straight stitches randomly over the gray felt using 2–3 strands of gray embroidery floss.

05 Pin the side and top edges of the body sections together, catching in the tail at one side. Sew through all layers using a simple running stitch, removing the pins as you go.

06 Glue the head to the top of the body, tipping it at a slight angle to add extra interest and character to the finished snow fox puppet.

07 To make the Inuit girl, use the templates to cut one face from cream felt, one hood from teal felt, one sweater and two sleeves from moss green felt, and two body pieces from black felt. Cut two semicircles from dark pink felt for her shoes and two small light pink circles for her cheeks. Make up in the same way as the snow fox, and use two beads for her eyes and a single strand of black embroidery floss for her nose and mouth. Cut scraps of jersey fabric and fringe the ends to make her scarf.

08 To make the penguin, use the templates to cut one face and one stomach from white felt, and one head, two flippers, and two body pieces from dark gray felt. Also cut two shallow semicircles from light pink felt for cheeks and two from yellow felt for feet, and a triangle of yellow felt for the nose. Sew on two bead eyes to finish.

SEE P94 FOR TEMPLATES

09 To make the polar bear, use the templates to cut one head, one snout, and two body pieces from white felt. Also cut a black felt triangle for the nose and round off the edges. Sew on bead eyes and embroider the leg division and "claws" with a single strand of black embroidery floss.

10 To make the reindeer, use the templates to cut one head and two body pieces from light brown felt, two dark brown antlers and a cream stomach. Cut a small red circle for the nose. Embroider on the closed eyes, and stitch small horizontal running stitches on the stomach (in gray) and head (in cream).

TIP
To cover the back of your stitches and give a neater finish, glue an additional piece of felt over the back of the snow fox's head and tail pieces after you've sewn on the fur texture.

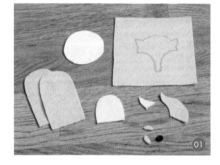

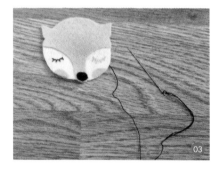

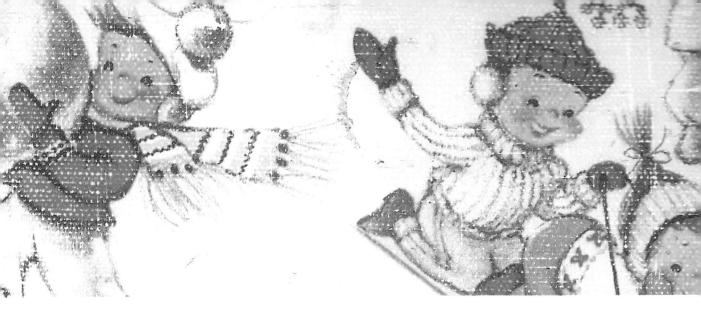

TWO TO KNIT
BERIBBONED CUSHION

THIS CO-ORDINATING CUSHION COVER AND LAVENDER SACHET FEATURE A STRIKING BUT SIMPLE TO KNIT STITCH PATTERN. MADE IN SOFT, NEUTRAL COLORS AND FINISHED OFF WITH CONTRASTING RIBBONS, THESE ARE IDEAL PRESENTS COMPLETE WITH THEIR OWN GIFT-WRAP BOW!

CHOOSE TO KNIT BIG OR SMALL!

HOW TO MAKE ... BERIBBONED CUSHION

MATERIALS: PILLOW COVER

TWO 100ɢ BALLS (219 YARDS/200 METERS) OF ROWAN CREATIVE LINEN, IN STRAW #622 OR SIMILAR YARN (DK-WEIGHT LINEN/COTTON BLEND)

KNITTING NEEDLES, ONE PAIR OF SIZE 8 (5 ᴍᴍ)

TAPESTRY NEEDLE

FABRIC, ABOUT ½ YARDS/0.5 METERS

SEWING THREAD IN MATCHING COLOR

SEWING NEEDLE

IRON

CUSHION PAD, 17³/₄ x 17³/₄" (45 x 45 ᴄᴍ)

NARROW RIBBON, ABOUT 2¼ YARDS/ 2 METERS

GAUGE TIP
The project features garter stitch, which is quite stretchy so gauge is less important here, as long as the knitted square fits the cushion cover.

HOW TO MAKE ... THE PILLOW COVER

01 Making the knitted part.
With size 8 knitting needles and holding the yarn double, cast on 55 sts.
Rows 1–10: Knit.
Rows 11–96: K8, (k1, yo, k2tog) thirteen times, k8.
Rows 97–105: Knit.
Row 106: Bind off.
Weave in loose ends. Press the piece to make it even all over.

02 To make up the cushion, start by cutting the fabric so it measures 19 x 44¼" (48 x 112.5 cm) – don't worry if the length is not exact.

03 Double fold and press one short end by 1" (2.5 cm) and hand-sew the hem.

04 Fold over the other short end by 17³/₄" (45 cm) and press. Now fold the hemmed end over to give you the cushion cover shape and press again. Open the fabric out and fold in each of the long sides by ⅝" (1.5 cm) and press.

05 Turn the fabric over and hand-sew the knitted piece onto the cushion front (center panel) so it sits in place. Turn the fabric back to the wrong side, place the cushion pad in the centre panel and refold as step 4. Slip stitch the sides of the fabric together, catching in a small part of the knitted piece to make it hold. To finish, wrap the ribbon around the cushion and tie in a bow.

VIBE ULRIK SONDERGAARD

Danish knit designer Vibe Ulrik Sondergaard studied fashion design and photography. She currently works as a designer, producing hand-knitted swatches that are sold to fashion companies in New York, Los Angeles, Paris, Barcelona and London. Vibe's colorful, textured designs are both practical and beautiful.

MATERIALS: LAVENDER SACHET

ONE 50G BALL (142 YARDS/130 METERS) OF ROWAN PIMA COTTON DK, IN LOZENGE #055 OR SIMILAR YARN (DK-WEIGHT 100% PIMA COTTON)

KNITTING NEEDLES, ONE PAIR OF SIZE 2/3 (3 MM)

TAPESTRY NEEDLE

FABRIC, 6 x 12" (15 x 30 CM)

SEWING NEEDLE

DRIED LAVENDER

NARROW RIBBON, ABOUT 16" (40 CM)

TIP
The distinctive stitch pattern is made by teaming together an increase, made by a yarnover (yo) with a decrease (k2tog).

HOW TO MAKE ... THE LAVENDER SACHET

01 Make front part of sachet. Using size 2/3 knitting needles, cast on 25 sts.
Rows 1–10: Knit.
Rows 11–44: K5, (k1, yo, k2tog) five times, k5.
Rows 45–53: Knit.
Row 54: Bind off.

02 Make back part of sachet. Using size 2/3 knitting needles, cast on 25 sts.
Rows 1–53: Knit.
Row 54: Bind off.

03 Weave in loose ends. Press the piece to make it even all over.

04 To make up the lavender sachet, put the front and back knitted pieces together, wrong sides together, and sew three of the seams.

05 Fold the fabric in half and sew two sides together to make a pocket. Turn the "pocket" inside out to hide the seams and fill with dried lavender. Sew together the final seam and put the flower-stuffed bag into the knitted sachet.

THE LAVENDER SACHET MEASURES 5 x 5" (13 x 13 CM)

06 Sew the last seam of the knitted sachet closed. Weave in any loose yarn ends. Finally, wrap the ribbon around the sachet and tie in a bow.

Abbreviations

k: knit
k2tog: knit two stitches together (decrease by one stitch)
st(s): stitch(es)
yo: yarnover

MACHINE-EMBROIDERED
CHRISTMAS PICTURE

FREEHAND MACHINE EMBROIDERY IS A GREAT WAY TO CREATE A FESTIVE PICTURE. SIMPLY PLACE YOUR MOTIFS ON A BACKGROUND FABRIC AND USE YOUR MACHINE NEEDLE AS YOU WOULD A PEN TO CREATE REALLY INTERESTING STITCHED DETAILS. YOU WILL NEED TO LOWER THE FEED DOGS ON YOUR MACHINE AND USE A DARNING/EMBROIDERY FOOT.

HOW TO MAKE ... CHRISTMAS PICTURE

SEE P93 FOR TEMPLATES

MATERIALS

TWO PIECES OF CONTRASTING FABRIC FOR THE BACKGROUND, ABOUT 9 x 19" (23 x 48 CM) FOR "GROUND" AND 10½ x 19" (27 x 48 CM) FOR "SKY"

BATTING, ABOUT 14 x 18" (35 x 46 CM)

FABRIC SCRAPS OF YOUR CHOOSING FOR THE PICTURE MOTIFS

SEWING THREADS: RED, BROWN, AND YELLOW

FABRIC SPRAY ADHESIVE

EMBROIDERY HOOP, 9" (23 CM)

WATER-ERASABLE FABRIC PEN

SEWING MACHINE

DARNING/EMBROIDERY FOOT

FABRIC SCISSORS AND SMALL EMBROIDERY SCISSORS

01 Pin the two pieces of background fabric together horizontally, with right sides facing, to make a square piece of fabric. The "sky" area will make up the top two-thirds of the piece and the "ground" the bottom third.

02 Machine stitch using a ⅝" (1.5 cm) seam. Press open the seam, turn over to the right side and press the piece well along the seam line.

03 Cut a piece of batting to the same size as the background and pin to the wrong side of the fabric. Fix the fabric in the hoop by placing the inner hoop under the background fabric on the wrong side and the outer hoop over the top of the inner hoop on the right side, ensuring that there is a little more "sky" than "ground". Attach with the top screw piece of hoop. Remove any pins.

04 Enlarge the picture templates and cut out of paper. Pin the templates to the wrong sides of your chosen fabric scraps and cut out, ensuring that the shapes will be facing the right way once placed with right sides facing on the background fabric.

05 Spray the back (wrong side) of each picture piece with spray fabric adhesive in a well ventilated area. Place in position with right sides facing up on the background fabric.

06 Using a darning/embroidery foot on your sewing machine and with the feed dogs in the down position, freehand machine embroider the motifs, using two lines to outline each piece with red sewing thread.

07 Continue to add the detail to the picture. Use brown thread for the reindeer's eye and collar, and the reins leading to the sleigh. Use red thread for the reindeer's nose. Embroider red and yellow baubles on the trees and red bows on the parcels. Trim the loose ends of thread at the front and back of the work after sewing each piece.

08 When all the picture pieces are stitched in place, trim the edges of the background fabric allowing about 2–4" (5–10 cm) from the edge of the hoop. Add a loop for hanging.

TIP

If possible use a Perspex foot so you can see through it to the fabric. Keep the needle in the automatic stop-down position, so if you need to take a stitching break the needle won't go off track.

02

05

NICKI TRENCH

Nicki Trench is dedicated to the revival and promotion of home crafts. She is a prolific writer of craft books as well as a lecturer and feature writer on patchwork, quilting, crochet, sewing, knitting, hen keeping and vegetable gardening. To find out more see www.nickitrench.com or visit her blog nickitrench.blogspot.co.uk

03

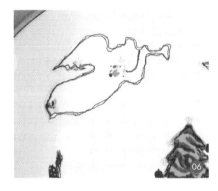

06

04

07

PAPER DECORATION

STRING OF STARS

MADE FROM PATTERNED PAPER, UPCYCLED BOOKS, AND A HINT OF SEASONAL SPARKLE, THESE PRETTY STAR GARLANDS OFFER A FUN ALTERNATIVE TO TRADITIONAL TINSEL OR PAPER-CHAINS. STRING THEM ACROSS A ROOM, A WINDOW, OR BETWEEN THE BRANCHES OF THE CHRISTMAS TREE TO ADD SOME STELLAR STYLE TO YOUR HOLIDAY DÉCOR.

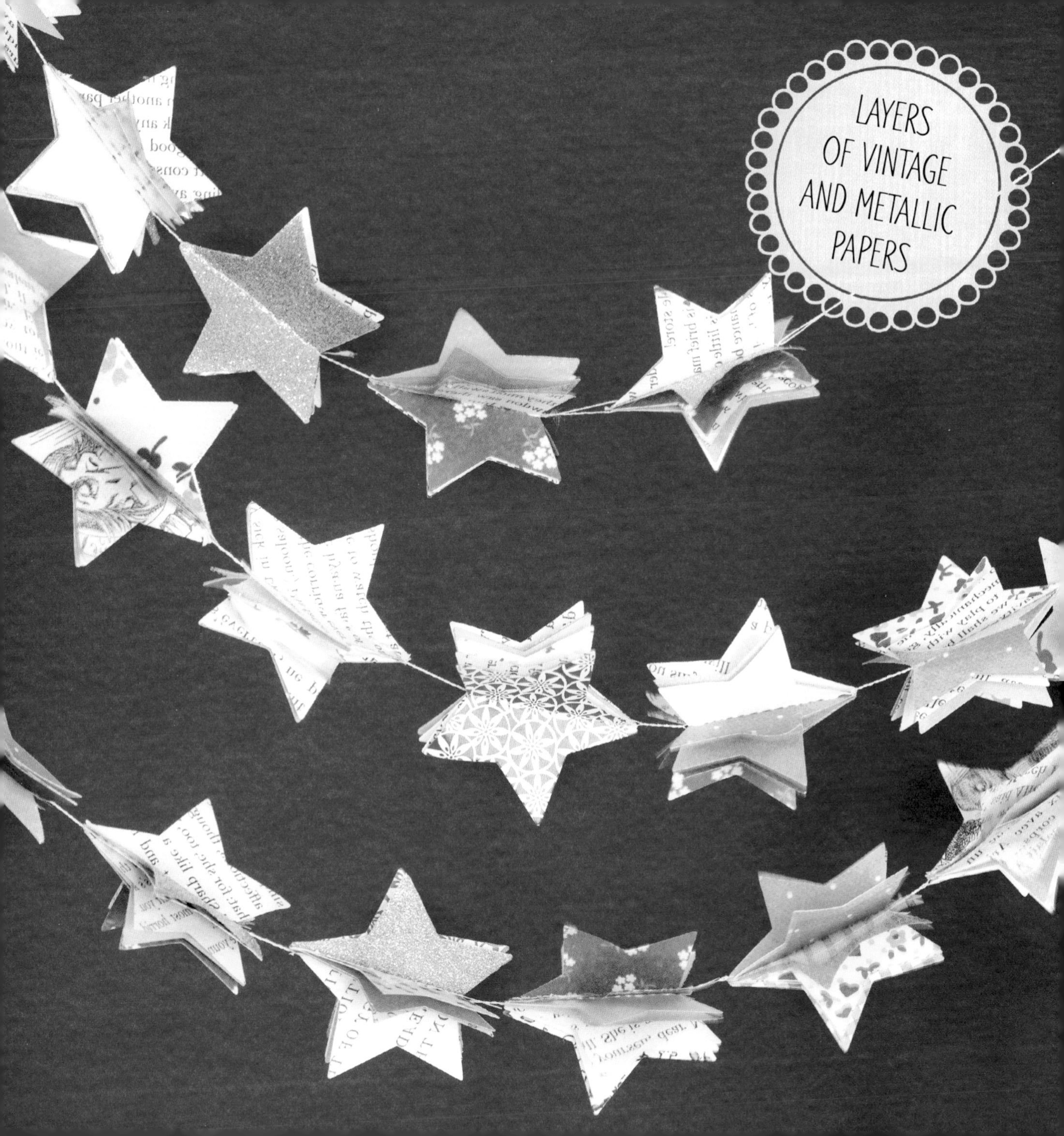
LAYERS
OF VINTAGE
AND METALLIC
PAPERS

HOW TO MAKE ... STRING OF STARS

MATERIALS

PATTERNED PAPER

OLD BOOKS

METALLIC OR GLITTER PAPER

WHITE SEWING THREAD

PENCIL

SCISSORS

SEWING MACHINE

01 Make a star template from cardboard and use to draw around this onto your chosen papers.

02 Bundle the stars together in groups of six. Alternate between the different types of paper and mix up the colors too.

03 Pull out a long length of bobbin and top thread from your sewing machine (this will make it easier to hang up your garland when you have finished). Align the edges of your first star bundle, then feed it through the machine, sewing along the center through all six layers.

04 When you reach the top, keep sewing for a couple of inches (a few centimetres) with nothing under the foot, then add your second star

TIP
You'll find it easier to sew through the paper bundles if you start at the base and stitch towards the top point of the star. Change your needle afterwards as sewing on paper will blunt it.

bundle. Stitch along the center as before.

05 Keep going, adding one bundle of stars at a time and leaving a small amount of "blank" thread in between. You can make these gaps an even size or vary them if you prefer.

06 When you're happy with the length of the garland, stop stitching and pull out another long length of thread as you did at the start. Snip the ends to release.

07 Finally, fold the layers of each star bundle gently along the stitched center line so that they splay outwards to create a pretty, dimensional paper star.

TIP
Look out for paper that is printed or colored on both sides so that your finished stars are beautiful from all angles. To save time, you could use a star punch or star-shaped die and die-cutter as an alternative to hand-cutting your stars.

DESIGNED BY KIRSTY NEALE

SEE P95 FOR TEMPLATE

01

02

03

04

05

SIMPLY STITCHED
CUTE CHARACTER NAPKINS

DRESS UP SIMPLE CLOTH NAPKINS FOR CHRISTMAS WITH THESE SWEET LITTLE CELEBRATORY MOTIFS HAND-EMBROIDERED ONTO BRIGHT FABRIC CIRCLES. CHOOSE A DIFFERENT COLOR CIRCLE FOR EACH, SO YOUR GUESTS CAN KEEP TRACK OF THEIR NAPKIN THROUGHOUT THE FESTIVE DINNER.

HOW TO MAKE ... CUTE CHARACTER NAPKINS

MATERIALS: PER NAPKIN

BRIGHTLY COLOURED COTTON FABRIC,
5 x 5" (13 x 13 CM)

EMBROIDERY FLOSS: WHITE AND COLORS TO
MATCH YOUR FABRICS

CLOTH NAPKIN

WHITE SEWING THREAD

WATER-ERASABLE FABRIC PEN

EMBROIDERY HOOP

EMBROIDERY NEEDLE

SCISSORS

PINS

IRON

01 Trace your chosen motif onto the
brightly colored fabric. Place the
fabric in the embroidery hoop to
keep it nice and taut as you stitch.

02 Using white embroidery floss,
embroider the design using six
strands for the main outlines and
three strands for the smaller details.
Use a backstitch for the outlines and
mouths, and French knots for the
eyes and berries (on the pudding).

03 Remove the embroidered fabric from
the hoop and trim to a 3½" (9 cm)
diameter circle, making sure that the
embroidery is centered in the circle.

04 Cut a 2¾" (7 cm) diameter circle
from paper and place in the center
on the back of the embroidered
fabric circle. Pin in place. Stitch a
large running stitch around the edge
of the fabric.

05 Pull the thread to gather the edges
in around the paper circle template.
Tie off the thread and then press.
Remove the template.

DESIGNED
BY MOLLIE
JOHANSON

06 Pin the fabric circle to the corner
of the napkin. With six strands of
matching colored embroidery floss,
sew a small running stitch around
the edge of the circle to secure it to
the napkin.

07 With three strands of colored
embroidery floss, sew a running
stitch border around the edge of the
napkin, stitching along the hem and
only catching the top layer.

TIP
By embroidering onto circles of
fabric not only do you identify
each person's napkin, but you also
keep your stitches hidden from
view. You could add matching
circle motifs along the edge of the
tablecloth too.

SEE P95 FOR TEMPLATES

Running stitch

Backstitch

French knot: bring needle up at 1, wrap floss around needle twice, then down at 2, holding floss taut around needle while pulling through the fabric.

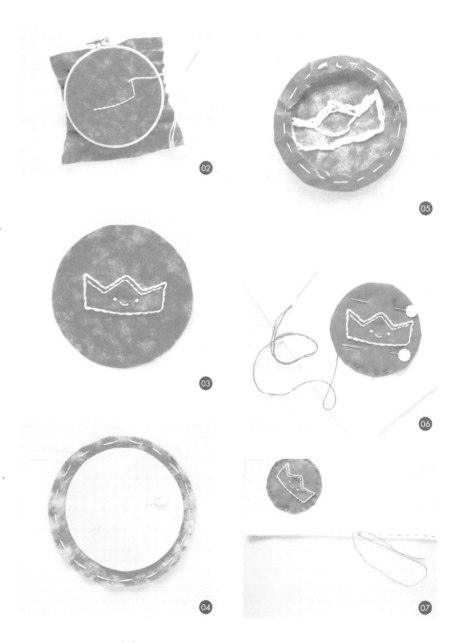

EASY FAIR ISLE
FINGERLESS GLOVES

THESE FINGERLESS GLOVES ARE JUST WHAT YOU NEED TO KEEP WINTERTIME CHILLS AT BAY. THE INTRICATE FAIR ISLE DESIGN ON THE BACKS OF THE GLOVES IS AN ATTRACTIVE TAKE ON TRADITIONAL PATTERNS, WHILE THE RIBBED SECTIONS AT THE PALMS HELP GIVE THEM A SNUG FIT.

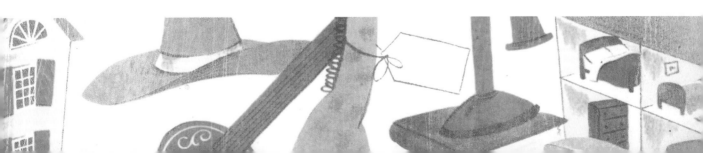

KEEP WARM
AND COZY

HOW TO MAKE ... FINGERLESS GLOVES

GAUGE TIP

26 sts and 38 rows to 4" (10 cm) square over St st using size 3 needles. Finished size laid flat: about 3½ x 8" (9 x 20.5 cm) after washing and sewing up.

MATERIALS

50G BALLS (246 YARDS/225 METERS) OF THE WOOL SHED ALBAYARN, ONE EACH IN SUMMER PUDDING (A), TEAL (B), LICHEN (C), LOCHAN (D), SPRING (E), MOSS (F), AND WINTER WHITE (G) OR SIMILAR YARN (4PLY-WEIGHT WOOL)

KNITTING NEEDLES, ONE PAIR OF SIZE 2/3 (3 MM) AND ONE PAIR OF SIZE 3 (3.25 MM)

TAPESTRY NEEDLE AND GLASS-HEADED PINS

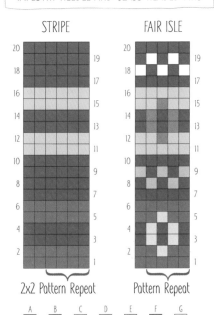

STRIPE   FAIR ISLE

2x2 Pattern Repeat   Pattern Repeat

A   B   C   D   E   F   G

01 Reading the Fair Isle chart.

The back of the gloves features a Fair Isle design. Use two colors at the same time across a row, following the color sequence from the chart below left. Each square represents a stitch; each horizontal line a row. Read the chart from the bottom right corner: knit or right-side rows run from right to left; purl or wrong-side rows from left to right. The design features a 20-row pattern repeat that is knitted twice, then the first 6 rows are repeated again (46 Fair Isle rows in all).

02 Understanding the pattern.

The gloves are knitted flat, then seamed together. The cuffs are knitted in a 2x2 rib. Once the cuff is complete, work the section that forms the back of the glove, including the Fair Isle panel, in St st, while continuing the palm in rib. The thumbs are made in rev St st.

The Fair Isle design for the right glove is worked at beginning of the row; for the left glove, it comes at the end of the row. When working a Fair Isle pattern you hold two color yarns at the same time; simply "float" or carry the color not in use across the back of the row. This design is worked so you do not have to carry the color over more than 3 sts.

03 Make the right glove from the cuff.

Using size 2/3 needles and yarn A, cast on 54 sts (see stripe chart).

Row 1: K2, *p2, k2, rep from * to end.
Row 2: P2, *k2, p2, rep from * to end.
These 2 rows form the 2x2 rib pattern; rep the last 2 rows a further 8 times (18 rows in total).

04 Knit the main part of the right glove.

Change to size 3 needles.
Row 1 (RS): K2, *p2, k2, rep from * 5 more times, M1, k to end of row. 55 sts
Row 2 (WS): P31, k2, *p2, k2, rep from * to end.

Carry on working 26 sts in 2x2 rib, working stripes as set out on the stripe chart, while the 29 sts of the St st section sets up the Fair Isle panel (see Fair Isle/FI chart).

Change to yarn B but do not break off yarn A.

Row 3 (RS): K2, *p2, k2, rep from * 5 more times, work row 1 by working in knit to the end of the row.
Row 4 (WS): Work as follows:
Join in yarn C at beg of this row to keep the fabric even. Insert RHN into first st purlwise, then bring up yarn C and place it across yarn B.

Next, work the first 2 sts as you would normally. The contrast yarn should now be caught behind the main color. Drop yarn B, pick up yarn C and work the next st as FI chart, then cont in this way until all the sts on the chart have been worked.

Complete the row using yarn B as follows: p2, *k2, p2, rep from * to end. Cont working 2x2 rib pattern and working from FI chart as set until row 13, using colors below for rib section.

Rows 5–6: Yarn A.

Rows 7–8: Yarn B.

Rows 9–12: Yarn A.

05 Place the thumb.

Join in yarn E but do not break off A. On the next row, start to increase for the thumb using M1: pick up the strand between sts by inserting your RHN from the back to the front of the strand, then insert your LHN from the back to the front under this loop and slip over onto the LHN, then purl as usual.

Row 13: K2, *p2, k2, rep from * 4 more times, p1, M1, p1, k2, work row 11 of FI chart. 56 sts

Row 14: Work row 12 from FI chart, p2, k3, p2 *k2, p2, rep from * to end (work rib in yarn A).

Row 15: K2, *p2, k2, rep from * 4 more times, p1, M1, p1, M1, p1, k2, work row 13 of FI chart. 58 sts

Row 16: Work row 14 from FI chart, p2, k5, p2, *k2, p2, rep from * to end (work rib in yarn E).

Row 17: K2, *p2, k2, rep from * 4 more times, p1, M1, p3, M1, p1, k2, work row 15 of FI chart. 60 sts

Row 18: Work row 16 from FI chart, p2, k7, p2, *k2, p2, rep from * to end.

Row 19: K2, *p2, k2, rep from * 4 more times, p1, M1, p5, M1, p1, k2, work row 17 of FI chart. 62 sts

Row 20: Work row 18 from FI chart, p2, k9, p2, *k2, p2, rep from * to end (work rib in yarn A).

Row 21: K2, *p2, k2, rep from * 4 more times, p1, M1, p7, M1, p1, k2, work row 19 of FI chart. 64 sts

Row 22: Work row 20 from FI chart, p2, k11, p2, *k2, p2, rep from * to end (work rib in yarn B).

Row 23: K2, *p2, k2, rep from * 4 more times, p1, M1, p9, M1, p1, k2, work row 1 of FI chart. 66 sts

Row 24: Work row 2 from FI chart, p2, k13, p2, *k2, p2, rep from * to end (work rib in yarn A).

Row 25: K2, *p2, k2, rep from * 4 more times, p1, M1, p11, M1, p1, k2, work row 3 of FI chart. 68 sts

Row 26: Work row 4 from FI chart, p2, k15, p2, *k2, p2, rep from * to end (work rib in yarn B).

Row 27: K2, *p2, k2, rep from * 4 more times, p1, M1, p13, M1, p1, k2, work row 5 of FI chart. 70 sts

Row 28: Work row 6 from FI chart, p2, k17, p2, *k2, p2, rep from * to end (work rib and thumb in yarn A).

Row 29: K2, *p2, k2, rep from * 4 more times, p16, turn.

Next row (WS): K15 – work on these 15 sts only to create thumb.

Work a further 11 rows in rev st st. Bind off knitwise.

Break off yarn, leaving length of yarn and use to sew down thumb seam until you reach yarn B.

06 Continue glove as follows.

With RS facing and using yarn A, pick up 2 sts at base of thumb, k2, then work row 7 from FI chart. 57 sts

Row 30: Work row 8 from FI chart, p2, k4, *p2, k2, rep from * to end of row.

Row 31: K2, *p2, k2, rep from * 4 more times, (p2tog) twice, k2, work row 9 from FI chart. 55 sts

Row 32: Work row 10 from chart, p2, *k2, p2, rep from * to end.

Keep working 2x2 rib at beg of row and the Fair Isle patt as set on rem 29 sts until a further 16 rows have been completed. Change to size 2/3 needles.

Break off yarn B and use yarn A for the next 3 rows and the bind-off.

Next row: K2, *p2, k2, rep from * 5 more times, k2tog, knit to end. 54 sts

Next row: K30, p2, *k2, p2, rep from * to end.

Next row: K2, *p2, k2, rep from * 5 more times, knit to end.

Bind off in rib for 26 sts, then bind off knitwise to end.

Abbreviations

beg: beginning

k: knit

LHN: left-hand needle

M1: make 1 (increase by one stitch)

p: purl

rem: remaining

rep: repeat

rev St st: reverse stockinette stitch

RHN: right-hand needle

st(s): stitch(es)

St st: stockinette stitch

HOW TO MAKE ... FINGERLESS GLOVES (CONTINUED)

DESIGNED BY CAROL MELDRUM

07 Make the left glove.
Work as right glove until cuff completed.
Work main part of glove as follows:
Row 1: K28, M1, k2, *p2, k2, rep from * to end. 56 sts
Row 2: P2 *k2, p2, rep from * 5 times, p to end.
Join in yarn B but do not break off A.
Row 3: Work row 1 of FI chart, k2, *p2, k2, rep from * to end.
Row 4: P2, *k2, p2, rep from * 5 times, work from row 2 of chart.
Cont working in patt from the FI chart and 2x2 rib as set until row 13, using colors indicated below for rib section.
Rows 5–6: Yarn A.
Rows 7–8: Yarn B.
Rows 9–12: Yarn A.
Work rib in yarn E.
Row 13: Work row 11 of FI chart, k2, p1, M1, p1, k2, *p2, k2, rep from * 5 more times. 56 sts
Row 14: P2, *k2, p2, rep from * 4 more times, k3, p2, work row 12 from FI chart (work rib in yarn A).
Row 15: Work row 13 of FI chart, k2, p1, M1, p1, M1, p1, k2, *p2, k2, rep from * 5 more times. 58 sts
Row 16: P2, *k2, p2, rep from * 4 more times, k5, p2, work row 14 from FI chart (work rib in yarn E).
Row 17: Work row 15 of FI chart, k2, p1, M1, p3, M1, p1, k2, *p2, k2, rep from * 5 more times. 60 sts
Row 18: P2, *k2, p2, rep from * 4 more times, k7, p2, work row 16 from FI chart (work rib in yarn A).

Row 19: Work row 17 of FI chart, k2, p1, M1, p5, M1, p1, k2, *p2, k2, rep from * 5 more times. 62 sts
Row 20: P2, *k2, p2, rep from * 4 more times, k9, p2, work row 18 from FI chart.
Row 21: Work row 19 of FI chart, k2, p1, M1, p7, M1, p1, k2, *p2, k2, rep from * 5 more times. 64 sts
Row 22: P2, *k2, p2, rep from * 4 more times, k11, p2, work row 20 from FI chart (work rib in yarn B).
Row 23: Work row 1 of FI chart, k2, p1, M1, p9, M1, p1, k2, *p2, k2, rep from * 5 more times. 66 sts.
Row 24: P2, *k2, p2, rep from * 4 more times, k13, p2, work row 2 from chart (work rib in yarn A).
Row 25: Work row 3 of FI chart, k2, p1, M1, p11, M1, p1, k2, *p2, k2, rep from * 5 more times. 68 sts
Row 26: P2, *k2, p2, rep from * 4 more times, k15, p2, work row 4 from chart (work rib in yarn B).
Row 27: Work row 5 of FI chart, k2, p1, M1, p13, M1, p1, k2, *p2, k2, rep from * 5 more times. 70 sts
Row 28: P2, *k2, p2, rep from * 4 more times, k17, p2, work row 6 from FI chart.
Row 29: Work row 7 FI chart, p16, turn.
Next row (WS): K15 – work on these 15 sts only to create thumb.
Work a further 11 rows in rev St st.
Bind off knitwise.
Break off yarn, leaving length of yarn and use to sew down thumb seam until you reach yarn B.

08 Continue glove as follows.
With RS facing and using yarn A, pick up 2 sts at base of thumb, p1, k2, *p2, k2, rep from * to end. 57 sts
Row 30: P2, *k2, p2, rep from * 4 more times, k4, p2, work row 8 from chart (work rib in yarn E).
Row 31: Work row 9 from FI chart, k2, (p2tog) twice, k2, *p2, k2, rep from * to end. 55sts
Row 32: P2, *k2, p2, rep from * 5 more times, work row 10 from FI chart (work rib in yarn A).
Keep working Fair Isle patt as set on 29 sts at beg of row then 2x2 rib until a further 16 rows are completed.
Change to size 2/3 needles.
Break off yarn B and use yarn A for the next 3 rows and the bind-off.
Next row: K27, k2tog, k2, *p2, k2, rep from * to end of row. 54 sts
Next row: P2, *k2, p2, rep from * 5 times, knit to end.
Next row: K30, *p2, k2, rep from * to end.
Bind off 30 sts knitwise, then bind off rem sts in rib as set.

09 Finishing off and making up.
Wash in tepid water, then squeeze out water gently. Place gloves on a padded surface, pin out Fair Isle section only to block, and leave to dry. Weave in loose yarn ends and sew up the side seams.

TEMPLATES

ALL THE SHAPES FOR THE BOOK'S MAKES. ENLARGE ALL TEMPLATES BY 200% BY PHOTOCOPYING THE PAGES, WITH THE EXCEPTION OF THE HEIRLOOM STOCKING WHICH SHOULD BE ENLARGED BY 400%.

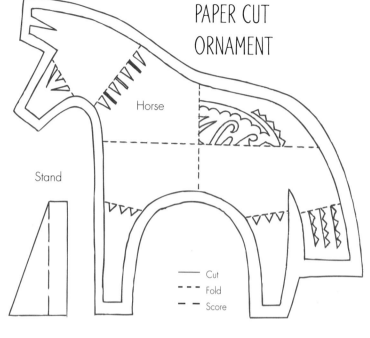

PAPER CUT ORNAMENT

Horse

Stand

—— Cut

--- Fold

— — Score

SHOPPING TOTE

CHRISTMAS PICTURE

FINGER PUPPETS

All Finger Puppets Body

Snow Fox Upper Head

Penguin Head

Snow Fox Lower Head

Penguin Face

Snow Fox Stomach

Snow Fox Tail

Penguin Stomach

Snow Fox Tail Tip

Penguin Flipper

Inuit Girl Face

Reindeer Antler

Inuit Girl Head

Reindeer Head

Inuit Girl Sleeve

Inuit Girl Sweater

Polar Bear Head

Polar Bear Snout

Reindeer Stomach

BAUBLE GIFT BAGS

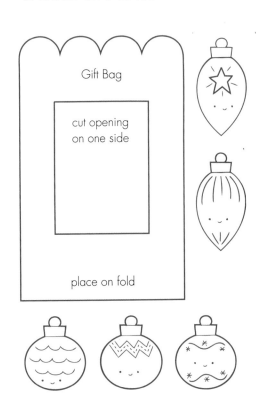

Gift Bag

cut opening on one side

place on fold

FESTIVE STATIONERY

DOOR WREATH

STRING OF STARS

HEIRLOOM STOCKING

Deer

Bauble

Collar

Nose

Ears

Eye

IPAD COZY

Oval

NOTE: THE HEIRLOOM STOCKING
TEMPLATES NEED ENLARGING BY 400%.

Main Stocking
(A)

CUTE CHARACTER NAPKINS

Stocking Top (B)

Toe (C)

Heel (D)

MORE GREAT GIFT BOOKS available from Interweave

INTERWEAVE PRESENTS CROCHETED GIFTS
Irresistible Projects to Make & Give
Kim Werker

ISBN 978-1-59668-107-1
$21.95

GIFTED
Lovely Little Things to Knit + Crochet
Mags Kandis

ISBN 978-1-59668-178-1
$24.95

For more information on *Mollie Makes*, please visit molliemakes.com

First published in the United States in 2012 by
Interweave Press LLC
201 East Fourth Street
Loveland, CO 80537
interweave.com

© 2012 Collins & Brown

ISBN 978-1-62033-101-9
Library of Congress Cataloging-in-Publication Data not available at time of printing.

10 9 8 7 6 5 4 3 2 1

Printed and bound in China by 1010.

PUBLISHER'S ACKNOWLEDGMENTS

This book would not have been possible without the input of all our crafty contibutors. We would also like to thank Cheryl Brown, who has done a brilliant job of pulling everything together, and Sophie Martin for her design work. Thanks also to Leah at KraftyChicDesigns (www.etsy.com).

Project photography by Rachael Smith, as follows: p7, 11, 13, 21, 25, 29, 35, 39, 43, 47, 51, 59, 63, 69, 73, 77, 81, 85, 89.

And of course, thanks must go to the fantastic team at *Mollie Makes* for all their help, in particular Jane Toft and Kerry Lawrence.